ENGLISH FOR ARGUMENTATIVE WRITING

John K. Swensson
De Anza College

Copyright © 2016 John K. Swensson

Publishing rights licensed to Chapter Apps Inc.

All rights reserved.

No part of this publication may be reproduced, stored in a retrieval system or transmitted in any form or by any means, electronic, mechanical, photocopying, recording, scanning, or otherwise, except as permitted under Section 107 or 108 of the 1976 United States Copyright Act, without either the prior written permission of the Publisher or authorization through payment of the appropriate per-copy fee to the Copyright Clearance Center Inc., 222 Rosewood Drive, Danvers, MA 01923, website www.copyright.com. Requests to the Publisher for permissions should be addressed to the Permissions Department, Chapter Apps, Inc., 1901 So. Bascom Avenue, #1180 Campbell, CA 95008 U.S., email contact@chapterapps.net. The Publisher may take legal action to enforce its rights. The Publisher may recover damages and costs, including but not limited to lost profits and attorney's fees, in the event legal action is required.

ISBN: 978-0-9967820-0-5

TABLE OF CONTENTS

UNIT 1: THE ARGUMENTATIVE APOCALYPSE	5-7
UNIT 2: EXAMPLES OF LITERATURE	8-13
UNIT 3: THE BODY PARAGRAPH	14-18
THE BODY PARAGRAPH: SLIDES	19-20
UNIT 4: THE ARGUMENTATIVE ESSAY	21-35
THE ARGUMENTATIVE THEME: SLIDES	36-37
UNIT 5: LOGIC & THE ESSAY	38-46
UNIT 6: DOCUMENTATION OF THE ESSAY / GRAMMAR GUIDE	47-49
UNIT 7: STUDENT SUCCESS	50-55
THE TEN YEAR LIFE PLAN: SLIDES	56-58
UNIT 8: CULTURAL CONSIDERATIONS	59-64
UNIT 9: EDITING SKILLS	65-71
UNIT 10: ANALYZING LITERATURE	72-80
THE ELEMENTS OF LITERATURE: SLIDES	81-84

UNIT 1: THE ARGUMENTATIVE APOCALYPSE

By John Swensson, swenssonjohn@gmail.com
Writing for FUN and Enlightened Understanding in the 21st Century

This text is designed to assist my students in their efforts to become great argumentative writers and speakers. It contains the material to assist you in a variety of English courses, both Composition and Literature. Thank you, the late Mike Hoffhines of Maui Community College and Apple, for teaching me how to make webpages, and Anthony Campbell, Javier Rueda, and Dave Garrido at De Anza College for great technical and other support. I am most in debt to thousands of wonderful students in my classes from whom I have learned so much.

Throughout the chapters that follow you will find many of those students' essays, as well as material from Jeanne Wakatsuki Houston who co-wrote, with her husband James D. Houston, the seminal FAREWELL TO MANZANAR, the story of US incarceration of its Japanese-American citizens during World War II. Jeannie's essay "A Tapestry of Hope" was the graduation address to a graduating class at De Anza College in Cupertino, CA, and is a master statement about the strengths of our diversity. It is **Unit 2** in this text which also contains a suggested reading list for a lifetime of reading, and a wonderful poem by Dana Gioia.

Unit 3 The Body Paragraph, addresses the basic unit of argument and how to write effectively. It is the most important Unit for you no matter what type of writing you are doing, and, if you are writing argument, Unit 4 is also an imperative. Units 3 and **Unit 4**, **The Argumentative Theme**, are both rather rather prescriptive, what we used to call at my undergraduate school, the US Military Academy at West Point, the M1A1 Argumentative theme. The beauty of this format is twofold: 1. It always works and 2, format being a given, you are free to think creatively and powerfully as you find and organize EVIDENCE to support your position. You no longer need worry about how to organize your papers.

Unit 5, Logic, covers how we think. I call it "Logic Light" as in one chapter it addresses Induction, Deduction and Fallacies. Once you have studied Unit 5, have some fun and do the exercise analyzing the logic in Andrew Marvell's "To His Coy Mistress," and also ask yourself why we have stereotypes.

Unit 6, Documentation covers the very important topic of documenting your sources using MLA, Modern Language Association, format. In some science courses or Speech you will need to use APA, American Psychological Association, format, but if you go to Easybib.com and select the correct format, you will be covered. The Internet certainly makes things easier to use the proper format. Unit 6 also contains a link to a grammar guide which is very helpful and a fun way to learn grammar and punctuation. If you have trouble with, for instance, run-on sentences (aka the comma splice) go to the section on that topic, download the fun PowerPoint and do the exercises.

Unit 7, Student Success, is what this text is all about, making YOU successful. Wherever you are, whether in school or not, success often involves finding and using assets that are around you and available to you. There are many ways to be successful, and persistence will pay off, and a good plan is often the key to future success. Unit 7 contains a Ten-Year Life plan in which I require my students to VISION where they want to be. Don't be held back by a limited vision or selling yourself short. You can be a US Senator or President, you can make a Hollywood movie, and you can be financially successful. But first you should write an Education Plan, a Work Plan, and a Lifestyle Plan to accomplish your goal. I give each of my students a mentor who has already accomplished what s/he wants to achieve. There are plenty of mentors around you: teachers, clergy, social workers, and successful people who are more than willing to share their experiences with young people.

Unit 8, Multiculturalism, is how we prevail in modern society. We live with each other, study with each other and learn from one another. Learning styles differ across cultures as do the treasures that one can bring to the table. Jeannie Houston's wonderful essay "A Tapestry of Hope" appears in Unit 2, and I encourage you to read it and reflect on what it says to you in your surroundings. It is the essence of the strengths of a diverse society. Technology really has shrunk the world and brings us together. Consider the recent earthquake in Nepal: We watched it on TV and the Internet, learned about the country and the Nepalese society and some of us found ways to contribute monetarily to recovery efforts. It was the bringing to our consciousness a culture we had not known before.

Unit 9, Peer Editing, explains a simple technique to helping you learn how to write. Simply by using ALL CAPS you can edit another student's paper or have your own

edited. No need for fancy softwares, though nothing wrong with editing software either. Don't be afraid to make a mistake—sometimes we learn more when we are wrong than right. So write a draft and then ask a fellow for a second opinion; ask her or him to peer edit your paper using ALL CAPS. And be tough. If you sugar coat a critique of a weak paper, you do the writer no favors. Nice editors finish last J Unit 9 also contains sample student papers and sample peer edits.

Unit 10, Analyzing and Writing about Literature, could be a book by itself. The title says that you will analyze and then write about literature. Critical judgment if you will—critical thinking (See Unit 5 above) about literature. I love John Ciardi's book title HOW DOES A POEM MEAN? Unit 10 will allow you to determine how any work of literature means and give you the tools to articulate an explanation of what is going on in a work of fiction, poem, short story, drama, or novel. Hopefully that will sharpen your appreciation of great literature and increase your enjoyment. A careful understanding of literature can also lead to a better understanding of yourself. **You** are what this text is about and you are what great literature is all about.

My Educational Philosophy is that students need to proactively get their education for themselves.

My teaching style involves lots of Collaborative Learning, a methodology that will require you to take responsibility for your education. Group Work plus good communications skills plus research and risk taking, practiced within a developing learning community will allow you to obtain the education you need. You will get that education, and live, in a highly multicultural world, a world which has been shrunk by technology, and by politics. It is imperative that you understand other cultures, as well as your own.

At the same time you need to be technology literate in order to prevail (as opposed to merely enduring to use William Faulkner's words) in the current millenium. In addition, I believe that you should strive for excellence in your education, and you must be a bit selfish to accomplish that-- you need to GET YOURS. Your challenge in your life-long learning is to now figure out how to succeed in a Community College and go to only two years of a great four-year school, then get your Masters Degree, etc. You need to figure out what your aptitudes and interests are, how to be admitted to a great school that will foster those, and how to fund that education. **You cannot afford not to go to a great school.** If you want to know which great school is best you for, and visit that school online, start your search at Princeton Review. If you

need or want a scholarship, go now, immediately to FASTWEB.Com, and start your individual scholarship search. Do not say, next life I will go to Harvard—Do it this trip; do it now!!!!

Two final thoughts from the dolphin:

WEAR YOUR SEATBELTS!

DON'T DO DRUGS!

Corrections/comments to swenssonjohn@gmail.com

UNIT 2: EXAMPLES OF LITERATURE

This Unit, Unit 2, contains the wonderful essay about multiculturalism by Jeannie Houston, a suggested "lifetime" reading list for your own education, followed by a great poem by Dana Gioia. Many of the works in the reading list are referred to in Unit 10, Analyzing and Writing about Literature, *et. Passim*.

"A Tapestry of Hope"
AMERICA'S STRENGTH WAS, IS, AND WILL BE ITS DIVERSITY
By JEANNE WAKATSUKI HOUSTON

Many Years Ago, 43 to be exact - when I stood on the ground where De Anza College now stands, I looked out onto lush orchards, fragrant with blossoms in springtime and laden with plump fruit in summer. I viewed acres of foliage carpeting the earth with green - patches of beans, tomatoes and squash, and long furrows of strawberries, glistening red under their leafy canopies. In those days I knew this area well, for I had spent several summers picking those berries at a large strawberry ranch called Esperanza, located not far from here. Esperanza, the Spanish word for "hope," was farmed by Japanese families in partnership with the Driscoll brothers. They were sharecroppers. My father sharecropped with the Driscolls at another ranch in South County from 1951 to 1955.

In 1945 when our family re-entered society after three and a half years of incarceration at Manzanar, a concentration camp for Japanese-Americans during World War II, my father's fishing license was revoked. It forced him to seek a livelihood outside a successful pre-war fishing occupation.

Starting at economic zero, at age 59 he seized the opportunity to begin again and brought his family to San Jose from Southern California to farm strawberries. Although my father had been in this country for more than 35 years, and his family, including my mother, had been born here, we arrived at this luscious valley like new immigrants, refugees from another world.

Why do I tell you this? I tell you this because when I picked those berries I never dreamed I would be speaking at a college that someday would rise up within view of where I knelt in the dirt. It was beyond my imagination. But here I am sharing with you some thoughts and insights I have accrued since those days in the strawberry fields more than 40 years ago.

As Santa Clara Valley's landscape has changed, so has its consciousness. I'm not going to lecture about how tough it was then to be Asian, to be poor, and to be a woman. But I would like to say a few words to remind us how we have changed, how things are different - especially in attitudes toward ethnic diversity.

When I was growing up in the '50s, being "American" and acceptable into mainstream society meant one had to assimilate, melt into one great pot where the broth was predominantly Anglo-European flavored.

No one talked about the concept of cultural diversity as a mosaic or as a tapestry of multi-colored threads that when woven together created a vibrantly rich and textured fabric. "Real Americans" were white. People of color had to think and act "white" to prove their "Americanness." And while I was growing up after the war, muted by the internment experience, it never occurred to me to question this attitude.

Not even when I was told I should not continue with a journalism major at San Jose State because I was "Oriental" and a female. There were no jobs in the field. So I changed my major to social welfare. And when I was told again by the head of Juvenile Probation Services that they could not hire me as a probation officer because the community was not "ready" for "Orientals," I did not protest - although I had been educated enough by then to know it was wrong. But that was the '50s.

Equal opportunity laws were non-existent. I remained silent, returning to the safety zone of invisibility and "don't make waves" mentality.

Rediscovering our Histories

Then in the '60s, the Black Power movement changed forever the way racial and ethnic minorities thought of themselves. Black leaders led us to rediscover our cultural backgrounds and our histories. We rediscovered our participation in and our contributions to the development of this country, and with this recognition came a sense of pride and identity.

For the first time in U.S. history, an awareness of values inherent in America's sub-cultures rose into public consciousness. We began to see that when individuals have a strong sense of identity, of pride in one's heritage, this sense of self-worth strengthens the larger society. Not only were attitudes changing in the dominant culture, but also sub-groups themselves began to recognize that America is a land of immigrants, and that all immigrants had a hand in developing it.

Thirty years ago, the word "immigrant" seemed reserved for people of color, individuals from the Third World. Today, this still seems to be the prevailing myth. I hear so often the comment, "America is becoming - so multi-cultural with all this immigration from Asia and south of the border." Some people are surprised or mystified or threatened by this idea that the country is becoming so diverse, when in fact, it always has been.

From the moment Portuguese and Italian sailors landed in the New World to mingle with indigenous peoples in what we now call the West Indies, America began its cross-cultural heritage. And up North, more than 500 indigenous tribes, speaking as many different languages, for centuries had lived on this vast and fertile continent.

Ethnicity is not the exclusive property of people of color. We all have ethnicity. We are descendants of individuals from China, Ireland, Ethiopia, Vietnam, El Salvador, Canada - to name a few.

Ideally, Americans should not have a problem with identity; we must realize there is no need to "wanna-be ethnic" --because, in fact, we all are.

"The World is Watching"

I would like to share an experience I had two years ago when I was in Japan. I met a Japanese man, a visionary who founded a grass-roots movement called "the Sweet Potato Movement." It was a calling back to the land from the cities, the dense urban areas he referred to as the "fourth world."
He surprised me with this comment, "The world is watching America deal with its diversity. For the Japanese, America is the role model for democracy. We may be strong economically, but we need your country to lead us in human rights and values. You must succeed if democracy is to succeed around the world."
He was one of many Japanese I met who saw multi-culturalism as a pivotal test for America's democratic ideals.
I like to view our diversity as a metaphor, a microcosm of the macrocosm of a world of nations. I like to see America as a great experiment, a laboratory for testing ideals - the big test today being tolerance and cooperation. If we can't get along in our own communities because of our cultural differences, how can we expect nations around the world to co-exist peacefully?
One of our greatest challenges is to embrace our differences while seeking out the common bonds that hold us together. What are those bonds? What are those threads, the warp in the loom that sets the pattern for who we are as Americans? For me, those threads are the ideals of freedom, equality, opportunity, justice. I also include the human qualities of gratitude, generosity, curiosity and love. Those threads together provide the strength and foundation around which our individual cultural differences weave, making each and every one of us unique and interesting Americans.
As I noted earlier, there was a major shift in perception to reach the point of agreement that we are, indeed, a multi-cultural society, that we began with diversity. But there is a difference between cultural diversity and cross-cultural understanding. They are not synonymous. The great opportunity now is to seek out ways to enhance cross-cultural understanding and not fall back on separatism and attitudes of "our tribe against theirs."

The Search for Scapegoats

Today, in a time of economic crisis, there are those in our political leadership who are all too ready to find scapegoats.

More and more, it seems, those scapegoats are immigrants. The voices of fear echo daily on the front pages of newspapers, in our television broadcasts: "They are different from us. They have no idea of democracy and freedom. They won't speak our language and they keep to themselves."

Those are the words used today to describe the newest Americans. How many of us who lived through the racism and internment of Japanese-Americans during World War II remember what it was like to have those words directed against one innocent group.

In 1942, we had no one to speak up for us. But after the war, empowered by the Civil Rights movement of the '60s, Japanese-Americans began a 10-year drive for redress from our government.

It culminated with the passage of the Civil Liberties Act of 1988, which officially apologized for the internment-- Japanese-Americans were vindicated in the eyes of history. But this victory was not for Japanese- Americans alone. It was a great victory for all Americans, for it proved our Constitution is not just a piece of parchment under glass in the National Archives. It is a living, vital contract that binds us all together as Americans.

And if that contract is broken - as it was in 1942 - it is not just the rights of individuals that are threatened, but the very fabric of this nation. And we know that the fabric is woven from threads representing many different groups. If one of those threads is cut, stretched out of proportion, or bleached of color, the design becomes listless and in danger of unraveling.

I began this talk with a memory, a powerful memory, which should underline one of the ironic possibilities of living in America. Who knows what the future holds for any of us? But whatever measure of success we have achieved is because we own a certain capacity. That capacity is hope.

When I was a teen-ager picking strawberries on that ranch, so appropriately named "Esperanza," I did not have vision. I could not envision the future I have today. Yet, I did have an unexplainable pull to fulfill some possibility, some unknown challenge. I now know that urge to fulfill was hope, a submerged belief in my own power, in the possibility I could accomplish "something."

Today I salute the accomplishments of all people and their faith - their faith in themselves and thus, in a future for this country.

(Thanks to the author for permission to use this piece in our classes and in this textbook. This was first delivered as the graduation address to the De Anza College Class of 1994 on 17 June, 1994-jks)

SUGGESTED READING LIST

Here follows a suggested reading list of great works that can inform your life and bring you great joy and entertainment. They are presented chronologically from date of first publication.

Du, Nguyen. THE TALE OF KIEU. Trans. Huynh Sanh Thong. New Haven: Yale University Press, 1984. This is the best English translation available and comes in paperback with Vietnamese on one side and English on the other. First published around 1815, this is the central epic of the Vietnamese Culture. If you wish to understand the Vietnamese people, this is the key to that understanding.

Hawthorne, Nathaniel. "Young Goodman Brown." A short story in many anthologies. First published in 1835, it is the greatest look into the nature of good and evil, and their combination (in the pink ribbons) that we have. Hawthorne and Faulkner, and perhaps Fitzgerald, will still be here 500 years from now.

Fitzgerald, F. Scott. THE GREAT GATSBY. 1925. The Great American Novel. All you need to know but AFTER you read it, compare or contrast the 1974 film with Robert Redford with Baz

Luhrmann's bombastic 2013 version. Enjoy. Read the book every ten years to measure your own change.

Faulkner, William. AS I LAY DYING. Various editions. First published in 1930. This is the easiest entry into the great works of Faulkner and if you like it, then read SANCTUARY, and then the two greatest works, THE SOUND AND THE FURY and ABSALOM, ABSALOM. "I used to think Hope was all man had, and then I realized that was all he needed—jest hope." W.F.

Houston, Jeanne W. and James D. Houston. FAREWELL TO MANZANAR. Many editions and also available in video. First published in 1973, this is the great revelation of America's incarcerating its own citizenry for no other reason than their original family country of origin. Don't understand Sunni vs. Shia? We did not understand our own Japanese-American citizens.

Yukio Mishima "Patriotism." First published in 1961 by the Japanese ultranationalist teacher and writer, this short story is one of the bloodiest love stories written. It is the extreme case of loyalty to one's country. Mishima writes of ritual disembowelment or Seppuku, which he then committed, having his students cut off his head. I do not allow that in my classes.

Erdrich, Louise. LOVE MEDICINE. I prefer the first edition from 1984, though she has rewritten and republished it twice. The story of two families on a reservation, the Kashpaws and the Lamartines, it is a wonderful, refreshingly written novel of Native American culture.

Boublil and Schoenberg's astounding musical LES MIS based on Victor Hugo's novel LES MISERABLES. The English version first appeared in 1985. Best versions are available from PBS on YOUTUBE—The Ten Year Anniversary Dream Cast done in 1995 with Colm Wilkinson as Valjean or the 25 year Anniversary released in 2011. Skip the movie adaptations--none of them make it. Enjoy the music. The Ten Year Anniversary has had 6 million views for good reason. It is my favorite and will be yours too. ENJOY!

Salter, James. BURNING THE DAYS. This 1997 memoir by a great American writer is a riveting accounting of the stories of his life as a West Point cadet, fighter pilot in Korea, film writer, expatriate, father and husband. It was my privilege to nominate him for the Nobel Prize in Literature. This is his greatest work. A modern day Faulkner. At the age of 92, he published a sex novel—but the greatest in this genre is his A SPORT AND A PASTIME.

Hosseini, Khaled. THE KITE RUNNER, First published in 2003 and set in Afghanistan. Hosseini was a medical doctor working for Kaiser Permanente until he published THE KITE RUNNER which spent 101 weeks on the New York Times bestseller list. A great modern American novel, from a wonderful writer and humanist.

READING POETRY

I love poetry, and my favorite poets are Wallace Stevens (A Life Insurance executive), John Crowe Ransom (a Southerner), Edwin Arlington Robinson (A New Englander whose "Richard Cory" is probably the great American poem as GATSBY is the GAN), and Dana Gioia. A Californian who was a former advertising Executive for Jello and Vice-President of General Foods—I taught his work in my Advertising Class also—he was for five years the very effective Chairman of the

National Endowment for the Arts (NEA) and with X.J. Kennedy is the co-author of LITERATURE;

AN INTRODUCTION TO FICTION, POETRY, DRAMA, AND WRITING, currently in its 12th Edition.

With Dana's permission, his wonderful poem below is a tribute to his firstborn son, Michael Jasper Gioia, who died in infancy. As I lost my daughter also, the poem has particular meaning to me. We read literature to understand ourselves—See also Unit 10. Thank you, Dana.

"Planting a Sequoia"

All afternoon my brothers and I have worked in the orchard,
Digging this hole, laying you into it, carefully packing the soil.
Rain blackened the horizon, but cold winds kept it over the Pacific,
And the sky above us stayed the dull gray
Of an old year coming to an end.

In Sicily a father plants a tree to celebrate his first son's birth–
An olive or a fig tree–a sign that the earth has one more life to bear.
I would have done the same, proudly laying new stock into my father's orchard,
A green sapling rising among the twisted apple boughs,
A promise of new fruit in other autumns.

But today we kneel in the cold planting you, our native giant, Defying the practical custom of our fathers,
Wrapping in your roots a lock of hair, a piece of an infant's birth cord,
All that remains above earth of a first-born son,
A few stray atoms brought back to the elements.

We will give you what we can–our labor and our soil,
Water drawn from the earth when the skies fail,
Nights scented with the ocean fog, days softened by the circuit of bees.
We plant you in the corner of the grove, bathed in western light,
A slender shoot against the sunset.

And when our family is no more, all of his unborn brothers dead, Every niece and nephew scattered, the house torn down,
His mother's beauty ashes in the air,
I want you to stand among strangers, all young and ephemeral to you,
Silently keeping the secret of your birth.

from The Gods of Winter © 1991 Dana Gioia

UNIT 3: THE BODY PARAGRAPH

Objectives

To learn the parts of a Body Paragraph.

To learn the qualities of an effective Topic Sentence.

To learn the qualities of an effective Body Paragraph.

Discussion

THE BODY PARAGRAPH

THE BODY PARAGRAPH is so named because it eventually becomes the body of your argument. A body paragraph may stand alone, or it may become one of many paragraphs in a longer essay. Its component parts are the TOPIC SENTENCE, EVIDENCE, and ANALYSIS; it may also contain a RESTATED TOPIC SENTENCE at its conclusion. So there are three (or four) parts to the Body Paragraph.

THE TOPIC SENTENCE-R,U,P

Usually you write the TOPIC SENTENCE as the first sentence in the paragraph in order to immediately tell your reader what you are going to argue. The Topic Sentence is an OPINION & should be well focused--or RESTRICTED, and UNIFIED, and PRECISE (RUP). A Topic Sentence in argumentative writing is not a fact--it is an opinion.

RESTRICTION means that you have settled on a well-focused, manageable aspect of an argument that can be supported with specific evidence, either from personal experience or outside sources. You cannot successfully argue in one body paragraph that a Toyota is better than a Mazda; you will have better luck if you limit your argument in that paragraph to a restricted aspect such as handling, or economy, or appearance, or performance. A well-restricted topic will be supported by specific evidence. The two major keys to effective argumentation are RESTRICTION and EVIDENCE, and the narrowness of the topic will result in better specificity of evidence. Think small!

UNIFIED means that there is only one idea in your topic sentence. Similarly all of the evidence in that paragraph should be about, or support, the topic sentence. The assertions that you have a good attitude and will work very hard in college do NOT support a topic sentence about your previous education; they are UNITY errors, since the Topic Sentence commits you to arguing about your previous education, not your present resolve. Look for the dreaded word "and" in a

TS, or a complex sentence; either condition may result in a lack of unity. PRECISE means that your topic sentence precisely states what it is you are going to argue in that paragraph. Precision may be a function of restriction; it is always a function of clear thought. "I have strong feelings about smoking" is imprecise and a statement of fact; "Smoking is harmful to your physical health" is more precise (and is an opinion).

The EVIDENCE that supports the TOPIC SENTENCE is the key to an effective paragraph. EVIDENCE typically consists of FACTS, STATISTICS, or EXAMPLES, and not opinions. The more concrete and specific the evidence, the more interesting and convincing the argument. Do not say you read books, or even novels in high school; say you read Herman Melville's MOBY DICK and F. Scott Fitzgerald's THE GREAT GATSBY in Mrs. Zacunga's 12th Grade Literature class at Overfelt H.S.

ANALYSIS, or logic, is YOUR OWN explanation of HOW the EVIDENCE supports the Topic Sentence. In the Toulmin Argumentative model, Stanford professor Stephen Toulmin calls analysis a "Warrant." The criticality of analysis may be seen in the example of a famous football player's trial. From the same evidence: the blood samples, the dark knit cap, the dog's barking, the Bruno Magli shoeprints, the thump on the wall that Kato Kaelin heard, and the gloves, etc., the defense argued "innocent," and the prosecution argued "guilty." Diametrically opposed topic sentences from the same concrete, specific evidence [intentional frag].

QUALITIES OF AN EFFECTIVE BODY PARA-UOCC

The four QUALITIES of a good body paragraph are UNITY, ORDER, COMPLETENESS, and COHERENCE. The mnemonic is U,O,C,C. Unlike RUP, the noise made by a frog, nothing makes this noise. But put this information in your brain housing group--commit it to memory. The reason I ask you to memorize these terms is that you will make extensive use of them in editing your classmate's papers, and you need, therefore, a common vocabulary.

UNITY

We started our discussion of UNITY in talking about that as a characteristic of the TOPIC SENTENCE (only containing one idea), and of the relationship between the EVIDENCE and the TS. There should be one and only one controlling idea in a paragraph. Discard evidence that is not central to, or directly supportive of the claim made by the topic sentence. A caution, however: do not discard concrete details that will make your paragraph more concrete, more interesting.

ORDER

The order of the evidence is crucial to an effective, coherent paragraph. Common orders in argumentative writing include STRONG-TO-STRONGEST (Why not weakest to strongest?),

CHRONOLOGICAL, and SPATIAL. STRONG-TO-STRONGEST is generally what YOU will make the most use of in this course. CHRONOLOGICAL order might be appropriate if your evidence occurred over a long period of time and you wanted to help your reader keep the evidence in a logical sequence. You would use SPATIAL(e.g. front to back or left to right) if you were arguing that a physical structure, such as a classroom ("This classroom sucks!"), were not up to standards, and a Spatial coverage would assist in your reader's understanding.

COMPARISON/CONTRAST is another type of order that we will cover later in the course.

COMPLETENESS

COMPLETENESS is a subjective, but critical judgment. A complete paragraph is well-developed and contains enough evidence to support the argument in the Topic Sentence. The answer to the question of whether a paragraph is complete, is adequately developed, is whether you have "ENUF" evidence and "enuf" analysis to prove the point in the topic sentence. You must have at least two items of evidence in a paragraph and 3-4 is more common.

COHERENCE

COHERENCE is a quality that means a paragraph flows smoothly and logically. "Order" and "coherence" are closely related. A well-ordered paragraph is probably a coherent paragraph. The use of pronouns is very important in creating coherence, and the lists of Transitional Words such as "first," "moreover," " of even greater importance," and "in conclusion," should be used frequently to guide the reader through your paragraph. (See Unit 5, below for a list of transition words.)

Summary

The four COMPONENTS of a Body Paragraph are the TOPIC SENTENCE, EVIDENCE, ANALYSIS and, optionally, THE RESTATED TOPIC SENTENCE.(Mnemonic is "TEAR.") A good Topic Sentence is RESTRICTED, UNIFIED, and PRECISE. (Mnemonic is "RUP," the noise a frog makes.) The QUALITIES of an effective Body Paragraph are UNITY, ORDER, COMPLETENESS, and COHERENCE (Mnemonic is "UOCC.") Now YOU go write an effective, scintillating paragraph!

Lab
DISCUSSION QUESTIONS--THE BODY PARAGRAPH

As soon as you have been organized into groups, one person should read the question below aloud to all members of the group. Another person should serve as recorder, and take notes of the deliberations. Either the recorder or a third person should be the spokesperson for the group. WRITE SOME POINTS ON THE BLACKBOARD, OR, IF YOU HAVE TIME, MAKE A HANDOUT of the important points. Also, it is OK, within your group, to disagree. If you do not have a consensus in your group, any member of the group may state a minority opinion.

A. Explain the nature of ARGUMENTATION. While you do not have an assignment per se on this subject, college writing should be concerned with topics that are CONTROVERSIAL, WORTHWHILE, and RESTRICTED. Discuss what you believe each of these terms means, and be prepared to share--you may wish to outline on the board--some topics that you think are appropriate for a college course in argumentative writing. (Hint: also see G. below)

B. Explain TOPIC SENTENCES. The discussion above states that a Topic Sentence usually is the first sentence in a body paragraph. Some texts show them at either end of a paragraph, and one text even suggests they can go in the middle. Who is correct and why? Or is this a trick question? Write on the board (or handout) some examples of good topic sentences, keeping in mind the qualities of Restriction, Unity, and Precision.

C. Explain UNITY. One idea in a paragraph and every piece of evidence in that paragraph should support the topic sentence. Either from something you have already written --like your diagnostic paragraphs--or from your imagination, think of some Unity violations from the writing sample exercise. Is resolve for the future an appropriate piece of evidence to use in a paragraph that argues whether your previous education has prepared you to be successful in English class (Exercise 3.5.1, below)? Why is it not a unity error (or is it?) in that same paragraph to provide specific details about the appearance of a particularly favored or loathed high school English teacher?

D. Explain COMPLETENESS. Some texts call this "development," i.e. your paragraph needs to be well developed. The explanation of Completeness (3.2.6, above) says that in a body paragraph you have to have "ENUF" evidence to prove the assertion in yout topic sentence. In your own words, explain how much evidence you need to prove the point about your "previous education." Why do you think you must always have at least two items of evidence in a paragraph? What if you had only used one example in your paragraph? What if your topic sentence was "My previous education has prepared me to be successful in English class," and all of your evidence came from Mrs. Zacunga's 12th Grade American Literature Class?

E. Explain ORDER. List and explain three ways to order evidence in an argumentative paragraph and argue when each might be appropriate. What happens in an argument if you show your best evidence first? Cite three items of evidence from a paragraph with the Topic Sentence just cited in

D. (immediately above), and explain why you chose the order that you did. Why did a SuperStudent a few years ago suggest that weakest-to-strongest should be renamed strong-to-strongest? How many items of evidence should you have brainstormed to come up with the three you then ordered?

F. Explain COHERENCE. Using the lists and examples of transition words found on the Internet or in another text, explain how to use the words and why they are so important. Also explain the concepts of TRANSITION and PARALLELISM. How do pronoun references assist coherence--(pls provide at examples to illustrate your answers-feel free to consult outside sources or other texts)?

G. SHARPSHOOTER GROUP. You have free reign over any of the preceding questions. You may add to, disagree with, or supplement each group's report. Organize as you see fit. With respect to A, above, why do you think Abortion, Gun Control, and Capital Punishment are NOT good writing topics?

Exercises

EXERCISE 1. "The Previous Education" Body Paragraph

(Note: This assignment is often used as a diagnostic paragraph) In an essay entitled "Shame," Dick Gregory argues that he learned to be ashamed in school when he was victimized by a teacher. He also recounts the taste of library paste, something you may or may not recall from your own personal experience. In "The First Major Turning Point," a part of his autobiography, Malcolm X tells us that he similarly put down by a teacher who told him he could not be an attorney because he was an African-American. In great detail, he goes on to tell us how he learned to read in jail, reading the dictionary, a word at a time. He particularly remembered the word "aardvark." Write ONE double-spaced Body Paragraph of at least 150 words (no upper limit) that argues one of the following topic sentences: My previous education has prepared me to be successful in English.

OR

My previous education has not prepared me to be successful in English . Note: This effectiveness of this paragraph will rely on the quality and quantity of specific evidence (such as the library paste or the word "aardvark") that you put in it. Be concrete. Include name of your school and/or courses, names of teachers, titles of books and author's names, if appropriate to your response.
EXERCISE 2. The "Family Background" Body Paragraph.

Write ONE double-spaced Body Paragraph which argues one of the following Topic Sentences:

My family background has prepared me to be successful in English.

OR

My family background has not prepared me to be successful in English.

Again, your evidence will come from your personal experience. Erik Eriksen, the great 20th Century Psychologist, argues that your Identity=Heredity+Environment

In other words your own identity is the sum of environmental factors (such as in which culture your family lived, how they felt about homework, etc.) and factors of heredity (i.e. were your parents smart, tall, or ?). You may wish to RESTRICT your response to either culture or heredity. You may wish to RESTRICT to only covering one parent. Your choice.

THE BODY PARAGRAPH: SLIDES

See Unit 3, above.

BODY PARA-Parts & Pieces

- TOPIC SENTENCE
- EVIDENCE
- ANALYSIS
- (RESTATED TOPIC SENTENCE)

BODY PARA- QUALITIES

- UNITY
- ORDER
- COMPLETENESS
- COHERENCE

ORDER

- Contributes to Coherence
- Chronological Order

- Spatial Order

- Strong-to-Strongest

COMPLETENESS

- A minimum of two items of evidence

- Generally three to four items of evidence

- Contains "Enough" Evidence

- Convinces the Reader

COHERENCE

- See Order

- Use transition words

- Read paragraph aloud and listen for choppiness

UNITY

- All evidence in the Para contributes to the Topic Sentence

- Analysis keeps you "on track."

- See explanation in Unit 3, Homepage

UNIT 4: THE ARGUMENTATIVE ESSAY

Objectives

To learn the parts and pieces of The Argumentative Theme. (This is the Apocalypse, the most important lesson in an argumentative writing course.)

As a part of that Objective, you will learn the parts, pieces, and functions of the INTRODUCTORY PARAGRAPH, the CONCLUDING PARAGRAPH, and the TITLE.

(The Body Paragraph has already been covered, in extensis, in Unit 3.) You will also learn how to write an effective, easy OUTLINE for the Argumentative Theme.
Discussion

THE ARGUMENTATIVE THEME

The argumentative theme is the basic form of persuasion, or argument, that we will study. It works for any length paper, including research papers, although the number of paragraphs and subdivisions must be modified. It also may form the basis for an argumentative speech (also called a Speech to Persuade), something you use in college or in life. You may use this form of argument, either formally or informally, to convince others of your position, your thesis.

The M1A1 Argumentative Theme is more effective if it deals with a CONTROVERSIAL, WORTHWHILE, and RESTRICTED topic, and is only as effective as the evidence, logic, and personal analysis that go into it.

Its effectiveness is typically a result of its RESTRICTION; the smaller your focus, the more specific will be your evidence; the more convincing your argument. DO not attempt to wrestle with and subdue the entire elephant. Write only about that one small piece of the elephant's ear you can hang onto.
**"The best thesis is an affront to somebody, a fly in the facial ointment of all convention."
Sheridan Baker**
The PARTS and PIECES of the argumentative theme (of perhaps 5-700 words) would look like:

TITLE

INTRODUCTORY PARAGRAPH:

Introductory Statements (6-8 sentences)

Thesis

Plan Step

BODY PARAGRAPH(S):

Topic Sentence

Evidence

Analysis

(Restated Topic Sentence-optional)

CONCLUDING PARAGRAPH:

Restated Plan Step

Restated Thesis

Concluding Statements (3-4 sentences)

A research paper might consist of three (or more) sections, with body paragraphs in each section. The ten-year life plan Research Paper (see Exercise 4.5.2, below) contains three required sections: Your education plan, your work/jobs plan, and a lifestyle plan. Each section may have a brief introduction, and, might have a brief conclusion as well.
The Introductory Paragraph

The Introductory Paragraph consists of three parts, the Introductory Statement(s), Thesis Statement, and Plan Step. The PLAN STEP is a summary of the TOPIC SENTENCES of your BODY PARAGRAPH and always starts with the words "I say this because."

INTRODUCTORY STATEMENTS--This may be a specific, attention-getting observation, a quotation, or a very sharp piece of evidence. The Introductory Statements normally name the topic, indicate some restriction or focus, and set the tone of the paper. In a 500-750 word paper, they should usually be 6-8 sentences in length. They should NOT be glittering generalities, one over the world statements that are meaningless and bore the reader. Do not start by stating platitudes about the importance of education to a refugee; tell us about your own trip to this country. Concreteness and specificity may as well start in the introductory statements.

THESIS STATEMENT--The point you are arguing. An Opinion. Restricted, Unified, and Precise. The narrower your thesis, the more specific will be your evidence, the more effective your argument. The thesis statement is, however, more general than your topic sentences, because they support the Thesis.

PLAN STEP--A summary of your topic sentences. The Plan Step has a logical, because-therefore relationship with the Thesis. The Plan Step generally, usually, starts with the words, "I Say this because. . ." otherwise known as **ISTB**.

Here is a **SAMPLE INTRODUCTORY PARAGRAPH** written by a super student. Note how the parts and pieces are clearly identifiable, in part assisted with the use of the words "I say this be

cause," between the THESIS and the PLAN STEP. Note also that the plan step, though two sentences long, implies that there will be three body paragraphs:

TRANSCENDING CULTURAL DIFFERENCES

Their homelands were separated by half the globe. They experienced culturally different backgrounds. Their lifetimes are divided by 1900 years. This is the relationship between Jeanne Wakatsuki Houston and the Apostle Paul. These authors have never met, and yet some of their writings parallel each other in most illuminating ways. These ways literally bond us together as a human race. As Jeanne has asked, "What are those threads. . .the pattern for who we are as Americans" ("Tapestry"4c)? Overcoming cultural differences is a common thread in the writings of Jeanne Wakatsuki Houston and the Apostle Paul. I say this because although they were both put through trials, they were both motivated by faith and took it upon themselves to be of service to others. Moreover, they both promoted the equality of all people through their writings
The Body Paragraphs

The Body Paragraphs start with a **TOPIC SENTENCE** which is an opinion, and which is itself, Restricted, Unified, and Precise (Same criteria as Thesis Statement). The Body Paragraph contains **EVIDENCE** and an **ANALYSIS** of that evidence. **EVIDENCE** consists of facts which support the Topic Sentence, and the evidence is **ORDERED**, normally in either strong-to-strongest, chronological, or a spatial order. The Evidence is supported by your **ANALYSIS** in which you relate and explain the relationship between the evidence and the Topic Sentence. The criticality of analysis may be seen in a trial in which, from the SAME evidence, the prosecution argues "guilty," and the defense argues "not guilty." A Body Paragraph **may conclude** with a **RE-STATED TOPIC SENTENCE**.

THE QUALITIES OF AN EFFECTIVE BODY PARAGRAPH: An effective Body Paragraph is **UNIFIED** (contains only one controlling idea), **ORDERED** (see above), **COMPLETE**.

(Contains "enuf" evidence to prove the point in the Topic Sentence), and **COHERENT** (Flows smoothly because of transition words, consistent pronoun referents, and a logical order to the evidence). For a more detailed discussion of The Body Paragraph, see UNIT 3, above.

A SAMPLE BODY PARAGRAPH for the sample Introductory Paragraph quoted ABOVE about Jeanne Wakatsuki Houston and the Apostle Paul, written by a student, is:

Both Jeanne and Paul were confronted by many trials. During WW II, when Jeanne was seven years old, her family was placed in an internment camp in the desert in Manzanar, California. They remained incarcerated there for four years. Her entire family slept in only two small rooms, and were given only two thin army blankets each. Jeanne said, "It was bitter cold when we arrived, and the wind did not abate ("Arrival" 181-86). She also experienced difficulty in planning a career because of her ethnic heritage ("Tapestry"4c). Similarly, Paul was put through many trials because he was a Christian. For example, he was imprisoned twice, beaten with rods three times, and once even stoned. These are only a few of the hardships Paul faced. Although he suffered, he delighted in his weakness because this made it evident to him that there was a greater power supporting him through all that he did (II Cor. 11:23-25).

Please note four things about this excellent paragraph. First, go back up and look at the relationship between the TOPIC SENTENCE of the Body Paragraph, and the beginning of the PLAN STEP in the Introductory Paragraph. The PLAN STEP promises to argue how they were subjected to trials; the TOPIC SENTENCE delivers on that promise. Second, note that this paragraph is an excellent COMPARISON paragraph which argues similarities (See the highlighted word "similarly," above.)--as opposed to a paragraph which CONTRASTS differences between things. Third, while I discourage students from writing about religion, this paper does not violate that stricture because it stays in a historical context. But finally, and most important, note the **CONCRETENESS of the EVIDENCE** in the paragraph.

Order of Body Paragraphs/Acknowledging the Opposition (aka THE TOULMIN MODEL)

In Unit 3 we looked at the order of evidence in a paragraph and concluded that it could be ordered chronologically, strong to strongest, or spatially. The same is true for paragraphs. You may order them the same way.

Let us suppose however, that you have one paragraph that argues against your thesis. You feel that your argument will have more credibility if you ACKNOWLEDGE the opposite side of the argument. Or, using the success in English example above, let us suppose that your family background was poor preparation for success (Family always moving, English not spoken in home, parents always working, too tired to help with homework), but that your previous education was excellent preparation. Being a good student, you know it is not a good move to ride the fence, and so you decide to add a third paragraph that talks about your excellent attitude. Now you have a thesis that argues that you will be successful, one paragraph that runs counter to the thesis, and two that support it. Introduce the negative first in order to "acknowledge the opposition" (to use Prof Steven Toulmin's terms—he of Stanford U) and then order the remaining two paragraphs strong-to-stronger.

Comparison/Contrast Organization
"If we rightly estimate what we call good and evil, we shall see it lies much in the comparison." William Blake

First, we must adopt a common terminology, however. If we "compare" objects, we are proving that they are similar. If we "contrast" objects, we are proving that they are dissimilar. Blake was arguing that two seemingly dissimilar concepts are actually similar, and texts often schizophrenically talk about "Comparison and Contrast." In your paper you will normally either compare OR contrast, but not both. In either event you must decide whether to use the "Subject-by-Subject" organization or "Feature-by -Feature." Let us suppose you are contrasting two tennis shoes: Nike and Reebok. To arrive at your thesis that Nike is the better of the two, you considered seven different features, threw out the weakest four, and decided to write on the three features of Price, Appearance, and Durability (in that strong- to-strongest order).

If you write using the Subject-by-Subject pattern you would write first about Reebok and then Nike, using two body paragraphs. If you wrote using the Feature-by-Feature pattern, you would use three body paragraphs. The first would cover Price, the second Appearance, and the third Durability. Please reread what I just wrote and think about it. If you still have a question, email me ☺

The Concluding Paragraph

The Concluding Paragraph starts with a **restatement of your PLAN STEP**. Here you are restating and summarizing your argument. You do not need to do this verbatim, but do not skimp either. **I generally use one sentence per body paragraph here.**

Next, you **restate the THESIS**, and I generally do this verbatim. The entire paper has been spent arguing and supporting this point. No need to change it.

The concluding paragraph **ends with CONCLUDING STATEMENTS**. These three-four sentences may look back to your Introductory Statements in order to "frame" your paper, may state wider implications, and do provide a graceful exit. This is not the place to be introducing new material, however.

The **cardinal sin** of body paragraphs is to be **too cursory, too brief**. Avoid this by including all of the parts and pieces, and by writing effective closing statements.

If you follow the explanation of the body paragraph, you will see that at minimum, it is six sentences in length: One each for each body para, one for the restated thesis, and three sentences of graceful exit/wider implications and/or framing.

The Concluding Paragraph is the last thing the teacher reads before assigning the grade, the last thing the banker reads before deciding on granting the loan, the last thing your reader reads before deciding whether your argument is reliable. Last impressions count!

The Title

But so do first Impressions. **The title is short, sexy, provocative, and creates an immediate impression.** It should entice the reader to want to read your paper, and a working title can help you stay focused during your writing. The title is NOT a summary of your thesis. It may include some mystery. It may use some alliteration. If you are assigned to write a paper about Success in an English Class, the title SHOULD NOT BE "Success." I The title could be **"Tom's Triumph"** or **"Dan's Disaster"** or **"The Nguyen Dynasty's First Great English Writer."** Or **"Sex and the Single Writer,"** or **"Overfelt's Finest."** Take some risks and use your imagination in the title. As Gatsby says, "Let your mind romp like the mind of god." Be creative, and create some excitement.

OUTLINING the Argumentative Theme:

There are four parts to an Argumentative Theme OUTLINE. They are (1) The Title, (2) The Thesis, (3) Topic Sentences, and (4) Evidence, either listed or as complete sentences. An Outline, then, would look like:

TITLE

THESIS:

TOPIC SENTENCE 1:

EVIDENCE 1A

EVIDENCE 1B

TOPIC SENTENCE 2:

EVIDENCE 2A

EVIDENCE 2B

EVIDENCE 2C

TOPIC SENTENCE 3:

EVIDENCE 3A

EVIDENCE 3B

A COMPLETED OUTLINE would look like this:

OVERFELT's FINEST

THESIS: I will be highly successful in English class.

TOPIC SENTENCE 1: My family background has been intensive preparation for success in English class.

1A: My mother Nancy's PHD in Liberal Studies

1B: Family travel throughout Europe, Asia, and Africa--multicultural exposure [note: this evidence is merely listed]

TOPIC SENTENCE 2: My excellent education at Overfelt High School left me well prepared for success in this English xx class.

2A: Mrs. Sloan's sophomore Social Studies class exposed me to a host of cultures and ideas.

2C: Craig "the Ace" Stephan's great Honors English Class taught me to construct powerful, well-organized arguments.

2B: My study partners in Junior English class, Tommy Wang and Chi Nguyen, helped me to begin to understand Asian Literature (Cite our discussion of Li Po's poetry).

[note: this evidence appears in complete sentences, and the last example includes the start of analysis to help remind you why you included the evidence.]

As long as you have the required four parts, you may lay out the evidence however works best for you. Also note in the second body paragraph how easy it is to change the ORDER of your evidence. As I was writing this outline, I concluded that Ace Stephan's class was the strongest item of evidence, so I labeled it "2C."

DO NOT OUTLINE INTRODUCTORY and CONCLUDING PARAGRAPHS. (Think about the fact that 2/3 of each of these paras is already in our outline—no need to outline Introductory and Concluding paragraphs.)

Also note that an outline is a living document. As I write this outline I am already seeing new ways to RESTRICT based on the EVIDENCE. If this were my paper, I would start sharpening my evidence and focusing toward a more restricted thesis, e.g.: "I will be highly successful with the multicultural aspects of this English class.

Summary and Samples

The ARGUMENTATIVE THEME may be the most important tool you learn in college. That is why it is your educational apocalypse; that is why the title of this homepage. You can use the Argumentative Theme in many of your college courses, and in much of your life. Like a good movie which has a beginning, a middle, and an end, it contains an Introductory Paragraph, Body Paragraphs, and a Concluding Paragraph. It should start with a **great title**. The PARTS and PIECES look like this:

TITLE
INTRODUCTORY PARAGRAPH:

Introductory Statements (6-8 sentences)

Thesis

Plan Step
BODY PARAGRAPH(S):

Topic Sentence

Evidence

Analysis
CONCLUDING PARAGRAPH:

Restated Plan Step

Restated Thesis

Concluding Statements (3-4 sentences)

SAMPLE ARGUMENTATIVE THEME #1:

Here is a wonderful argumentative theme written by Anna McW in an EWRT 1A Class. This paper is similar to the outline of "Overfelt's Finest," above. Thank you, Anna.

A Successful Escape from New York

Everyone always hears about the horrors of New York and how it can be uncompromising and ruthless. Of course you've also been exposed to New York at its worst if you've seen the movies, RUMBLE IN THE BRONX or ESCAPE FROM NEW YORK. However, it's not the hostility or the apathy of New York that I chose to recognize or dwell on. Rather it is in the positive qualities, such as its institutions of academic and cultural excellence, as well as the strength and passion of its ethnic diversity that I chose to reflect on and identify with. How am I able to say this? It was in New York's environment that I grew up, was educated, and acquired a philosophy that has enabled me to be successful in life. I like to think of this as my victory story. A story of "escaping" from what could have resulted in a life of negativity to one of accomplishment and optimism... of being successful at anything I set my mind to, including English 1A. **I will be successful in English 1A. I say this because** I believe my New York background and my family's strong sense of values have helped mold my thinking and instill in me determination and perseverance. These attributes together with my attendance at two of New York's finest parochial schools have, in turn, provided me with an excellent base, laid the groundwork for future accomplishments, and prepared me to succeed academically.

Yes, my family background has prepared me to be successful in English 1A. However, it wasn't due to my parents' exceptional intelligence nor their academic credentials. Rather it was their belief in the importance of education, and in the encouragement and support they gave me while I was in school. Surprisingly enough however, their education consisted mainly of "hard knocks" as neither parent ever went past the ninth grade. My father, Andrew, was a self-educated machinist and my mother, Beatrice, a housewife. They decided early that their misfortunes would not become their children's, so education was made a priority in my family. Perhaps too, this was the reason both were so adamant about doing homework, studying, getting good grades and attending the "right" school. They believed New York's public education wouldn't give the foundation to be successful later in life, so it was decided that attendance at a parochial school was a "must." As we didn't have much money, I know their decision must have caused great financial hardship, especially since there were five children who were given an opportunity that will be forever remembered. Besides paying for private education, they also set the stage for the attainment of goals. My father applied that ideology to everything, and laid down the law regarding school, homework, and grades. It was my mom who helped us with our spelling and vocabulary lists, listened to our essays, and worked on our school projects. The only subject my father deemed note worthy of his time was math, and that was because my mom was horrendous at it! Yes, I'll always be thankful for their encouragement and support during my academic years. Not because they did everything perfectly but because they set the stage for me to succeed. [Intentional Fragment]

My previous education has also prepared me to be successful in English 1A. Although some may have mixed feelings about their early childhood educational experiences, I relished the learning opportunities offered me during those formative years. My attendance at two fine parochial schools gave me the scholastic foundation needed to succeed in life. Our Lady of Refuge Elementary school with its summer reading lists and dreaded book reports, impromptu spelling-bees, and Sister Agnes' drills on the grammatical analysis of sentence structure provided me with a strong base on which to build the academic aspects of reading and writing. Although I can still remember the woes of sentence diagramming, I will always be thankful for the structure, no pun intended, this experience gave me. It was here too that my love of reading was born and evolved. It didn't matter whether it was MADAME CURIE's biography, Edgar Allen Poe's THE TELL TALE HEART, or even a Harlequin Romance novel, the result was to excel that has remained with me to this day. Aquinas High picked up where O.L.R. finished. Even though my first experience at Aquinas began with Latin, I welcomed the adventure. It was in this class, after reading the ILIAD and the ODYSSEY, that I learned I could survive Latin and love mythology. Mythology, with its fairy tale stories allowed me to tolerate the tempestuous tirades of a teeny tiny tyrant named Sister William Anna, my Latin teacher. She was a bore and a pain, constantly breathing down my neck, insisting I retranslate the passages of Caesar's battles from Latin into English. But translate I reluctantly did and, while dreaming about mythology, survived two years of Latin. Junior and Senior years found me reading the classics: Shakespeare's OTHELLO, and ROMEO AND JULIET; Hawthorne's the SCARLET LETTER; Orwell's ANIMAL FARM and 1984...to mention a few. These readings, along with their analysis, were required to pass Finals and to graduate. But who was complaining? Not I. Although many years have passed since my attendance at these schools, it was there that I learned the tools to be successful in whatever I chose to do. My determination to succeed and the knowledge I acquired over twenty-five ago have prepared me for events such as attending De Anza to get my business degree, working for an International Trading Company, and now taking English 1A.

So there you have it in a nutshell. **My story of how and why I believe the structure of my family background together with my previous academic and educational background has prepared me to take and succeed in English 1A.** Though some may disagree and feel the aforementioned is not sufficient evidence to prove this, I still maintain that I will succeed! Can any of you doubt that what I say is true? Have you no faith even after I've told you that I was born and raised in a place where many dare not venture? Better yet, does anyone of you even dare? Before answering, please remember where I come from, and the fact that you never say never to someone from New York because you don't know where the next "Rumble" will be...!

SAMPLE ARGUMENTATIVE THEME #2:

Written by Wanda H, it contains excellent parenthetical notes and a wonderful Works Cited, which shows how you can get wonderful information off of the Internet. The requirement was to write an argument concerning stereotypes.

The thesis was almost too unrestricted for my preference, but she was able to successfully argue her thesis because of the quality of her evidence:

Why Aren't There More Female Computer Scientists?

"The demographics of this country are such that the United States will not have enough engineers and scientists unless underrepresented groups increase their participation" (Spertus 1). This is complicated by the fact that the percentage of female computer science students is increasing at a very slow rate and may even be decreasing. Over forty-nine-percent of all professionals in the

workforce are female, yet females only comprise about thirty-percent of employed computer scientists (Frenkel 2). Several studies have been done in an effort to determine the cause of this disparity. After all, "There is no reason why women should not make up half the labor force in computing . . . It's not as if computing involves lifting 125 pound weights" (Frenkel 3). The researchers have concluded that stereotyping plays a definitive role in discouraging women from moving into Computer Science. While it may seem surprising to discover that stereotyping is still prevalent in the enlightened nineties, it is nevertheless a fact. **Professional women in Computer Science often suffer from the ill effects of stereotyping. I SAY THIS BECAUSE** Stereotyping against women is first encountered in the common use of sex-biased software. A female's education is also colored by stereotyping which sometimes begins as early as preschool and continues through college. Finally, women also encounter the infamous "glass ceiling" as they climb the corporate ladder.

Women first suffer from the effects of stereotyping as they use sex-biased software. Charles Huff and Joel Cooper did research to find out why the computer "is more alluring to boys than it is to girls." According to their results, when software is designed specifically for girls, designers usually generate learning tools, whereas games are usually generated when software is designed for boys. When designing for the generic "student," games are usually the end result. This research suggests that "Programs written for students are written . . . with boys in mind." Huff and Cooper conclude that "It is not the computer, or even the software, that is at the root of the sex bias in software, but the expectations and stereotypes of the designers of the software" (532). In another study, Sara Kiesler found that men also dominated the covers of computer games. Upon examining the covers of computer games 28 men and 4 women were illustrated. On one cover, two women were playing Monopoly with two men, on another, a woman was depicted as a "very fat queen," and on the last cover there appeared a "princess in supplicating position on the floor" (157).

Women are also discriminated against at the college level. Henry Etzkowitz studied students at a leading research university and discovered a "sexual separation of scientists" (Frenkel 8). He found that certain areas of science are labeled as male or female disciplines, which leads each gender to avoid certain areas. Computer science theory and particle physics are pretty much "off limits" to women, whereas some male faculty consider natural language to be better for females. This is because natural language is closer to the traditional gender roles such as the "expressive role and typing skills in software." In "The Classroom Climate: Chilly for Women?" Bernice R. Sandler made several observations which indicate that both men and women are guilty of stereotyping: females are interrupted more than males; faculty members make eye contact with male students more often than with female students; faculty members are more likely to know and use the names of their male students rather than the names of their female students; and females are often asked fewer or easier questions than males. Sandler writes, "Singly, these behaviors probably have little effect. However, when they occur repeatedly they give a powerful message to women: they are not as worthwhile as men nor are they expected to participate fully in class, in college, or in life at large" (149).

Because of stereotyping, rising above the glass ceiling in corporate America is hard for women. This is due, in part, to the fact that "most of management is male and feels more comfortable dealing with other men"(Drakos). However, female behavior does not receive the same acceptance as does equivalent behavior exhibited by men. Sandler wrote "He is `assertive'; she is

`aggressive' or `hostile.' He `lost his cool,' implying it was an aberration; she's `emotional' or `menopausal.' Thus, her behavior is devalued, even when it is the same as his" (151). Women are often overlooked for promotions or raises because of this "negative" behavior, which keeps them in the lower echelons at large companies. An independent study reported in BUSINESS WEEK said that "while women started out with comparable pay, within 10 years they were 25% behind their male counterparts" (Frenkel 4).

As the research cited above indicated, software is generally developed for a male audience, thus locking in the inequities of the past .This type of stereotyping, coupled with the discrimination women face during their education, sets the stage for male dominance in the field of computer science and results in lower pay for women in the field. **Professional women in Computer Science often suffer from the ill effects of stereotyping.** Fortunately discrimination against women has decreased significantly since the turn of the century. However, as the researchers have shown, stereotyping still plays a detrimental role in software, schooling, and the professional careers of women.

Works Cited

Huff, Charles and Cooper, Joel. "Sex Bias in Educational Software: The Effect of Designer's Stereotypes on the Software They Design." JOURNAL OF APPLIED SOCIAL PSYCHOLOGY 17.6 (1987): 519-532.

Drakos, Nikos. "The Glass Ceiling." Translation initiated byellens@ai.mit.edu. Apr 6, 1994. Online. Internet. 17 Feb 1997.Available www:http://www.ai.mit.edu/people/ellens/ Gende...star3_2_8.html#SECTION00028.

Etzkowitz, associate professor of Sociology at SUNY Purchase, and visiting scientist, Department of Computer Science, Columbia University. Unpublished.Workshop presentation: "The Power of Paradigms" 1990.

Frenkel, Karen A. "Women and Computing." COMMUNICATIONS OF THE ACM Nov 1990: full text. Online. Internet. 17 Feb 1997. Available WWW: http://cpsr..org/cpsr/gender/ frenkel.cacm.womcomp.

H, Robert W. Peer Editor. Husband to the author of this paper. 19 Feb 1997: 2 hours.

Kiesler, Sara; Sproull, Lee; and Eccles, Jacquelynne. "Pool Halls,Chips,and War Games: Women in the Culture of Computing." PSYCHOLOGY OF WOMEN QUARTERLY 9 (1985): 451-462.

Sandler, Bernice R. "The Classroom Climate: Chilly for Women?" THE ACADEMIC HANDBOOK 1988: 146-152.

Spertus, Ellen. "Why Are There So Few Female Computer Scientists?"1991: full text. Online. Internet. 17 Feb 1997. Available WWW: http://snyside.sunnyside.com/cpsr/gender/Spertus_womcs.txt.

Lab
LAB EXERCISE 1

UNDERSTANDING THE OUTLINE. Write a brief paragraph explaining why you think I have suggested that you NOT outline the Introductory and Concluding Paragraphs. (Hint: Compare the parts and pieces of these paragraphs, immediately above, with the four-part outline, above.)

LAB EXERCISE 2

INTRO PARA FOR AN ESSAY ON SUCCESS. Look back at the two body paragraphs in Unit 3 concerning your previous education (Exercise 3.5.1) and family background (Exercise 3.5.2) Write an introductory paragraph for a complete argumentative theme based on the paragraphs you wrote- or would have written for those exercises. Note: this is an easier exercise if your response to both paragraphs

was the same, i.e. if both your previous education and family background did or did not prepare you to be successful In English class. If one were positive and the other were negative, and you were a good student who wanted to argue a unified thesis, and did not want to "ride the fence," what would you have to do to tip the balance? (Hint: See The Toulmin Model, above)

Exercises
EXERCISE 1--JOB or EDUCATION

This theme is probably your first full-length theme in this class. Remembering that effective college writing depends on controversiality, worthwhileness, and restriction, and that the key to an effective argument is the EVIDENCE of an argument, select one of the following topics, according to your passions:

A. Define a problem, or recommend a solution to a problem, related to your employment or recent past employment.

B. Define a problem, or recommend a solution to a problem, related to your current or future education.

C. I would entertain an alternate topic ONLY if presented, in writing (typed) by ___.

The challenge here is first to think widely and actively about whichever of the two topics is of more interest. There is a major restriction challenge implicit in each. Do not attempt to argue both a problem and a solution in the same paper. If you are arguing a solution, define the problem as a given in the introductory paragraph (and elsewhere). The key to success here is a super RUP Thesis supported by 2 or more RUP TS--all of which came from EVIDENCE that you considered and ORGANIZED. Remember the UOCC principles both within body paragraphs and among them.

Finally, in this essay, we will move from the realm of evidence from personal experience to also include evidence from research. You must use three outside sources in the completion of this requirement. These sources could include books, magazine, personal or email interviews with your boss, coworkers, or educational administrators or other faculty (highly encouraged), or material from the Internet. You will be required to include a Works Cited section at the end of your paper on a separate page, and to use parenthetical notes within the body of your paper.

A typed, Four Part OUTLINE of your argument is due _____. (The four parts-- memorize these-- are title, thesis, TS, and EVIDENCE). The complete PEC will be due _____. The final paper will be turned in _____.

I am looking for exciting, interesting, well--restricted papers with great evidence and incisive thinking. I think finally they should be papers that are worth reading, that really do deal with real- world issues that you feel strongly about. As Gatsby observed, "let your mind romp like the mind of god." And collaborate.

EXERCISE 2--TEN YEAR LIFE PLAN-RESEARCH (EWRT 1A Assignment)
"Preparing for the Millenium"

Theme Four is YOUR paper, your MAGNUM OPUS for the course. the paper itself, will be worth 150 points. Typed, double-spaced, the paper's minimum length is 6 pages (2000 words) with seven references, at least one of which will come from your course readings. There is no maximum length. It is a personal paper that precisely states your detailed GOAL for the year 20__ (Ten years from now!), and ARGUES convincingly how you are going to achieve your goal. The paper will contain three required sections: (Educ=1/2). (The thesis is that if you follow the three plans you will be successful in accomplishing your specific 10-year vision for your future.)

The EDUCATION PLAN will argue in detail where and when you are going to obtain such education as is necessary to achieve your goal. Why did you choose which college to transfer to? Where and why will you take your graduate work? Where will financing for this education come from? If you decide to take all of your education in the Bay Area, defend that geographic choice.

The WORK PLAN will argue in detail where you will work during this period and why. Work would probably support educational financing and career development. How will you get those jobs? In that respect, your GOAL will be stronger if you name a specific type and size of company (or a specific company) rather than just a career field.

The LIFESTYLE PLAN will argue in detail how you will live your life and why. Personal inventory, selection of marital status, alternative lifestyles, and responsibilities toward siblings or parents may enter in here. While this section may require less research, it should be precise and thoughtful. You may include any other sections that you feel you need such as a background section (considering your heredity and environment, a kind of personal asset inventory), real estate or investments, community

or religious activities,, service to others, passionate hobbies, sports, etc (or you may wish to include some of these in your LIFESTYLE PLAN.)

This is YOUR paper so you have free reign. You may write in the future tense or the past tense-- just be consistent and remember that this is argument, NOT FANTASY. Your choices will be tested for the quality of research and rationality within the context of the choice. If you choose mediocrity, you must defend that choice. If you are going to be a Fish Crier that is fine; but how can you BEST prepare yourself to be the BEST fish crier? Get a Life! (Good students will read Carl Sandburg's "The Fish Crier.")

EXERCISE 3--TRASK RELIABILITY

DEFINITION OF RELIABILITY:

"When we are sufficiently convinced of the believability of an argument to believe it, or act upon it, we say it is RELIABLE."
West Point Logic Lesson, ca. 1972

RELIABILITY DETERMINATION: Haunani Kay Trask, "From a Native Daughter" (Note: Parenthetical notes refer to REREADING AMERICA, 2nd ed. Trask's essay is available from a variety of sources.) The steps for an effective determination of RELIABILITY are in Unit 5 of this text.

This formal assignment confirms and expands what we have been discussing re the argumentative theme and our study of evidence and logic. This major paper is 750 words long minimum (equal to three pages double spaced) and will utilize three references, correctly documented according to the MLA standards outlined and exampled in Unit 6 of this text.

Repeating what you already have been issued. The SUBJECT is How reliable is Trask's argument that Western historians have "decultured" the Hawaiian peoples? "What better way to take our culture than to remake our image? A rich historical past became small and ignorant in the hands of the westerners. And we suffered a damaged sense of people and culture because of this distortion (573)."

The key to a successful response will be RESTRICTION. Suggestions for restriction include her discussion of Western historians and

Language (573 et. passim)

Songs (577-79)

Gavin Daws' THE SHOALS OF TIME (573-74) (A similar historian)

People and the Land (575 et. passim)

Any ONE of the Hawaiian Stereotypes (576)

Clearly you can restrict even further within one of these selections; you could for instance just discuss Hawaiian reactions to annexation, or the Great Mahele. You must use at least three outside sources. You may use the film ACT OF WAR with the following cite:

ACT OF WAR. Trask et. al. NaMaka o ka` Aina, 1993

You have a lot of leeway here. The key will be to think small. If you look at the Daws' work for instance, you need analyze only two or three passages--the ones cited by Ms. Trask--not the entire work.

THE ARGUMENTATIVE THEME: SLIDES

Argumentative Theme--Parts & Pieces:

- Title

- Introductory Paragraph

- Body Paragraphs

- Concluding Paragraph

- Works Cited

Argumentative Theme--Title:

- Not your thesis

- Short, catchy, exciting

- Entice your reader to WANT to read your paper

- Usually Written last

- If obscure meaning, explain in intro paragraph

    Argumentative Theme-- Introductory Para:

- 6-8 Sentences of Introductory Material--name your topic, indicate restriction, generate interest. May be a specific quotation or an item of evidence. AVOID GENERALITIES

- Thesis (Opinion, RUP)

- Multi-sentence Plan Step (Summary of Topic Sentence) which starts with "ISTB."

Argumentative Theme--Body Paragraphs

- See Unit 3

Pax Vobiscum

Argumentative Theme--Concluding Paragraph

- Restated Multisentence PLAN STEP (Topic Sentence Summary)--not necessarily verbatim

- Restated THESIS--verbatim

- 3-4 Sentence Concluding remarks-graceful exit-no new material-wider implications, etc. May look back to intro remarks to "frame" paper-or look back to title

BEST KIEU ESSAYS (outline)

"Morality" by Faten H.

- THESIS: K's initial refusal to betroth Kim, and her later acceptance, are acts of virtue

- PLAN STEP: ISTB even though it was an attempt to break a pledge, it was done for unselfish reasons. Further, K exhibited a tremendous amount of honesty and acknowledged her own mistakes. Lastly her reluctant submission showed compromise and placed other's wishes above her own

"Madame Luna" by Stacey L

- THESIS: The moon illustrates Kieu's strong will and pureness

- PLAN STEP: ISTB the moon portrays her beautiful appearance, describes her mental state, and witnesses her life events which show her determination to stay as she was.

UNIT 5: LOGIC & THE ESSAY

DEFINITION OF RELIABILITY:

"When we are sufficiently convinced of the believability of an argument to believe it, or act upon it, we say it is RELIABLE."

West Point Logic Lesson, ca. 1972

Objectives

To learn the nomenclature, uses, and implications for argument of Inductive Logic.

To learn the nomenclature, uses, and implications of Deductive Logic.

To learn to identify, and either avoid or use, fallacies.

To learn to evaluate arguments for their "RELIABILITY," and to learn the definition of that term.

Discussion

"People who like this sort of thing will find this the sort of thing they like."
Abraham Lincoln [On Logic?]

INDUCTION

Inductive Reasoning moves from specific to general. From the specific of what I have observed, I make an inductive leap and arrive at one of **two types of inductive inference:** a **generalization** or a **hypothesis**. See the Huxley article below for some good examples of Inductive logic. The green apples and silver spoons examples will help you to remember the difference between a generalization and a hypothesis. **Generally a thesis or a topic sentence is either a hypothesis or a generalization.**

The STANFORD ENCYCLOPEDIA OF PHILOSOPHY has a very good discussion of Inductive Logic at http://plato.stanford.edu/entries/logic-inductive/

DEDUCTION

Deductive logic moves from general to specific. The basic deductive argument consists of a **Syllogism**, containing

(1) a **Major Premise**

(2) a **Minor Premise**

and (3) a **Conclusion**.

The first of these, the Major Premise, is usually general and the second, the minor premise, is more specific and less debatable. A Categorical Proposition relates and explains the relationship between two categories of things.

MAJOR PREMISE: All Thursdays are School Days

MINOR PREMISE: (All) Today is Thursday

We most commonly encounter deductive arguments as **enthymemes**, deductive arguments that are missing one or more parts. When we arose this morning (Thursday), we immediately concluded "Today is a school Day." Here is an enthyeme in which only the conclusion is stated-BOTH premises are missing. See also the summary below of Huxley's (Unit 5) "The Method of Scientific Investigation."

An excellent discussion of deductive logic may be found at Dr. David Mesher's logic page at San Jose State University.
Thomas Huxley, "The Method of Scientific Investigation."

SUMMARY-from memory-JKS

This essay, published in the nineteenth century, contains the thesis that scientists and the common man (sexist language, but acceptable then) each use logic the same way. Huxley then discusses two types of INDUCTIVE INFERENCES: the GENERALIZATION and the HYPOTHESIS. In INDUCTIVE LOGIC, we go from specific observations to more general, not necessarily observed, conclusions.

Following that he discusses DEDUCTIVE LOGIC, in which we move from general to specific. The basic form of a DEDUCTIVE argument is a SYLLOGISM which consists of a MAJOR PREMISE (which may be a GENERALIZATION or a HYPOTHESIS), a MINOR PREMISE which is more specific, and a CONCLUSION, which, in a VALID deductive argument, is forced from the Major and Minor premises.
(Note: Huxley does not discuss the term "RELIABILTY," but we shall be much concerned with it. **A RELIABLE argument is one which you believe to be sufficiently true to believe, or act upon. You should commit this definition, and the capitalized terms, to memory, for the sake of the quiz, and for life.**)

Back to Huxley: In defining GENERALIZATIONS, Huxley discusses the example of the green apples. On going to a store and purchasing a green apple, he observes that it is sour. He goes to another apple in the same store and finds the same thing. He then goes to another store and buys a green apple and it is sour. From the observation of those three apples, he GENERALIZES that "All Green Apples are Sour Things." He believes he has sufficient EVIDENCE to make this GENERALIZATION. He then passes by a field and finds a green apple under a tree; it is green and sour. He then travels to America where he goes to a store and buys a green apple which is also sour. He now believes his argument to be even more RELIABLE. So, when he wishes to have an apple pie made of sour apples, he always buys green ones. He then goes to Molokai where he finds a green guava. . .no, I made that up. But, the RELIABILITY of a GENERALIZATION

depends on SAMPLE SIZE and the BREADTH of the sample. A GENERALIZATION relates and explains LIKE items of information, in this case, green apples.

Huxley next discusses HYPOTHESES which relate and explain UNLIKE items of information. He uses the example of the missing spoons and teapot. A woman

awakes and proceeds one morning to her dining room, where she discovers that her silver teapot and teaspoons are missing. She races to an open window which she had closed the night before. She sees a handprint on the windowsill and muddy shoeprints in her garden. She formulates a HYPOTHESIS that a robber has stolen her silver; believing this a RELIABLE hypothesis, she calls the police. Her hypothesis--which is not necessarily true, but which is reliable, relates and explains UNLIKE items of information: missing spoons, missing teapot, open window, handprint, and shoe prints. As usual the RELIABILITY of the argument depends upon the EVIDENCE.

Huxley then discusses DEDUCTIVE logic including SYLLOGISMS. A sample is the best example:

MAJOR PREMISE : All persons are mortal

MINOR PREMISE: Socrates is a person.

CONCLUSION: Socrates is mortal.

In order for the conclusion of a Deductive argument to be reliable, the argument must be VALID, i.e. the conclusion must be forced from the premises, and the Premises themselves must be RELIABLE. The debate is usually centered around the MAJOR PREMISE, since it is more general, and is apt to be a GENERALIZATION or HYPOTHESIS.

Another example:

MP: All A is B

mp: All C is A

Conc: All C is B—Try drawing that VALID Argument. After you have drawn the two premises, the conclusion is ALREADY drawn.

Another example:

MP: No D is E

mp: All F is D

Conc: No F is E

Another Example:

MP: Most Asians are slow drivers.

mp: Nguyen is Asian

Conc: Nguyen is a slow driver.

The example immediately above is an example of a FALLACY, an error in reasoning. It is a sad example of stereotyping. What other kind of fallacy is this? The fallacy section, immediately following, may help you determine the correct answer.

FALLACIES

A fallacy is an error in reasoning. Generally, we should avoid fallacies, but that is not entirely correct, for often, as arguers, we make use of fallacies. The key to a critical thinking course is to be able to identify fallacies as they occur. The Nizkor WEB SITE, below, contains the following formal definition of fallacies, using terminology that is fairly similar to that which we shall use in class:

"In order to understand what a fallacy is, one must understand what an argument is. Very briefly, an argument consists of one or more premises and one conclusion. A premise is a statement (a sentence that is either true or false) that is offered in support of the claim being made, which is the conclusion (which is also a sentence that is either true or false).

There are two main types of arguments: deductive and inductive. A deductive argument is an argument such that the premises provide (or appear to provide) complete support for the conclusion. An inductive argument is an argument such that the premises provide (or appear to provide) some degree of support (but less than complete support) for the conclusion. If the premises actually provide the required degree of support for the conclusion, then the argument is a good one. A good deductive argument is known as a valid argument and is such that if all its premises are true, then its conclusion must be true. If all the argument is valid and actually has all true premises, then it is known as a sound argument. If it is invalid or has one or more false premises, it will be unsound. A good inductive argument is known as a strong (or "cogent") inductive argument. It is such that if the premises are true, the conclusion is likely to be true.

A fallacy is, very generally, an error in reasoning. This differs from a factual error, which is simply being wrong about the facts. To be more specific, a fallacy is an "argument" in which the premises given for the conclusion do not provide the needed degree of support. A deductive fallacy is a deductive argument that is invalid (it is such that it could have all true premises and still have a false conclusion).

An inductive fallacy is less formal than a deductive fallacy. They are simply "arguments" which appear to be inductive arguments, but the premises do not provided enough support for the conclusion. In such cases, even if the premises were true, the conclusion would not be more likely to be true. "

A good example of an inductive fallacy is a hasty generalization, a generalization that does not rest on a sample that is sufficiently large or have the breadth to support the inference. Perhaps that will answer the question about Nguyen, above. Other inductive fallacies include the Post Hoc fallacy, or post hoc ergo propter hoc, latin for "because of this, therefore that," also known as false causation.

While there are hundreds of fallacies, and you could easily spend an entire quarter studying the ones you will find in the following lists, ensure that, in addition to the inductive fallacies already mentioned, that you know:

Argumentum ad Hominem: rejecting or dismissing another person's statement by attacking the person rather than the statement.

Incorrect evidence from authority: citing the wrong authority, or material from an authority that is not relevant.

Overuse of the Argument of Emotion: explanation is self-evident.

Cultural fallacy: taking one's own culture as the standard of judgement

Red herring: introducing irrelevant material into an argument (Originally named for the technique of dragging a herring across a track to throw off pursuing dogs; your argument goes off in the wrong direction). Also known as the fallacy of diversion or irrelevance.

Non sequitur: offering a conclusion that does not follow logically from the premises.

Faulty analogy: assuming that because two things are similar in one respect, they are similar in all others.

All or nothing fallacy: things are either black or white; denies the grey area in between, or sets up a false dichotomy.

Circular argument or assuming what you are trying to prove--a fallacy I often use in argument; this makes the point that I am correct that fallacies are not necessarily to be avoided, but sometimes should be employed.

LISTS OF FALLACIES:

Real World Reasoning: A wonderful list of lists of fallacies, complete with links, masterfully done by Dr. Peter Suber, Department of Philosophy, Earlham College, in Richmond IN.

See Also:
http://www.earlham.edu/~peters/courses/inflogic/inflinks.htm

See also Copyrighted fallacy list of Dr. M. C. Labossiere at the Nizkor Site: http://www.nizkor.org/features/fallacies

TESTING FOR RELIABILITY

Technically, reliability is the degree of confidence that is placed in the truth of a proposition. When the evidence supports the conclusion in question to the extent that we are sufficiently convinced of its truth to act upon it, we say that the conclusion is reliable. For our purposes, a conclusion is simply reliable or not reliable. There are no pat mechanical rules for appraising conclusions for reliability, but there is a skill that can be learned and a systematic process that can be mastered which will help in making a reliable judgment. The analysis of any inductive prose argument should include the following steps:

Identify the conclusion (thesis) and the main supporting points (topic sentences)
Consider the inductive process
Identify any fallacies present in the evidence
Evaluate the evidence or the lack of evidence
Organize a defense for the judgment rendered

A. Identify the conclusion (thesis) and the main supporting points (topic sentences)

In the past you may have experienced difficulty identifying theses despite the fact that you have felt reasonably assured that these theses were stated somewhere in the introductory paragraphs. We will be concerned with identifying thesis statements and main supporting points in assigned readings. Additionally, we will be confronted with the problem of determining the theses in much of our research source material. Fortunately, in many cases, there are words and phrases called logical indicators which indicate that the writer has made an inference. These logical indicators focus on the inference and help to identify the conclusion. Each of the following words or phrases usually shows that the statement following it is a conclusion:

therefore

which shows that

proves that

hence

indicates that

consequently

you see that

implies that

entails

allows us to infer that

points to the conclusion

that suggests very strongly that

leads me to believe that

bears out my point that

from which it follows that

thus it can be seen that

Main supporting points are not always so easily identified; there are generally no indicator words. The structure of the argument is most often the key. Except in rather long essays or in those that are subtly sophisticated, the topic sentence of each paragraph is in fact a premise, and the information in the paragraph is the evidence which the writer has offered in support of that premise.

This first step in the systematic process can best be accomplished by diagramming the argument. The diagram provides a convenient pictorial representation of the argument which facilitates completion of the remaining four steps of the evaluation.

THESIS

TOPIC SENTENCE 1

Evidence in Body Para 1

TOPIC SENTENCE 2

Evidence in Body Para 2

TOPIC SENTENCE 3

Evidence in Body Para 3

Testing for Reliability is the critical task in our study of logic. Are we sufficiently convinced of an argument to believe it or act upon it? The rules of argumentation, evidence, and logic are all are key here. Your final task, having considered all of this, is to articulate your own well-organized argument as to whether an argument is reliable.

Below, you will find two favorites of mine, reliability evaluation of Andrew Marvell's poetic argument contained in "To His Coy Mistress," and the reliability of **just one** of Martin Luther King's eight arguments in "Letter from Birmingham Jail," namely,

King's claim that he is not an outsider. As you write this paper, you will see how key it is that you RESTRICT yourself to a portion of an argument that you can manage.

See also Exercise 4, evaluating the Reliability of Haunani Kay Trask's (activist in the Hawaii Separatist movement) argument in her essay, "From a Native Daughter."

English for Argumentative Writing

Summary

INDUCTIVE LOGIC moves from specific observations to more general, not necessarily observed conclusions, called INFERENCES. The two types of INDUCTIVE INFERENCES are GENERALIZATIONS and HYPOTHESES. GENERALIZATIONS relate and explain LIKE ITEMS. HYPOTHESES relate and explain UNLIKE items.

DEDUCTIVE LOGIC moves from GENERAL OBSERVATIONS (which may be Hypotheses or Generalizations) to more SPECIFIC CONCLUSIONS. The basic form of the Deductive argument is the SYLLOGISM, which consists of three parts:

The MAJOR PREMISE
The MINOR PREMISE
The CONCLUSION

If a Syllogism follows the rules of logic--which we shall not go into here--but, basically, if the Conclusion is forced from (or already contained within) the premises, the deductive argument is VALID.

We most commonly do not go around speaking in Syllogisms; rather we give only parts of a deductive argument. A deductive argument with one or more missing parts, is known as an ENTHYMEME. We also use chains of enthymemes.

RELIABILITY DEFINITION

When we are sufficiently convinced of the truth of an argument to BELIEVE it or ACT UPON it, that argument is, to us, RELIABLE. RELIABILITY does not necessarily equal truth.

Lab

LAB EXERCISE 1

STUDENT LOGIC CLASS, INDUCTION, DEDUCTION, and FALLACIES. In your assigned groups, be prepared to respond to the following questions, using your text (s), and the Huxley essay, "The Method of Scientific Investigation." The use of handouts or material written on the board is strongly encouraged.

GROUP A: Explain Inductive Logic and the Inductive inference known as the Generalization. On what does the reliability of a generalization depend? What is a hasty generalization? Where might you find a generalization in an argumentative essay?

GROUP B: Explain the Inductive Inference known as a Hypothesis. On what does the reliability of an hypothesis depend? Where do you normally find a hypothesis in an argumentative essay? What is the "Inductive Leap"?GROUP C: Explain Deductive Logic including the Syllogism. Find examples from everyday life to support the notion that we routinely use deductive logic. What does validity mean? What is the difference between reliability and validity? On what does the reliability of a valid deductive argument depend?

GROUP D: Explain Enthymemes and Fallacies. Why are enthymemes important, particularly since you went your entire life until now without hearing the word? If a fallacy is an error in logic, why might you want to employ one, or more?

GROUPS E & F: Explain Specific Fallacies, as assigned. In each case, try to come up with at least one example from outside your text. Also bring in any fallacy you might find from media advertising, such as an ad for women's cigarettes.

Exercises

EXERCISE 1, EVALUATING THE RELIABILITY OF AN ARGUMENT IN

ANDREW MARVELL'S POEM: "To His Coy Mistress."

ALL: When assigned, bring to class, a response to the following questions. You are encouraged to work together within your groups if possible:

A. What is the thesis of the poem, the main line of argument? Be precise. Look for indicator words, and see if structure is of any help also. B. What are at least two of the main supporting points (or Topic Sentences) and what evidence is introduced to support those? C. Do you feel the

evidence is strong and why? D. Put yourself in the place of the person to whom the argument is addressed. Is the argument RELIABLE? Why or Why Not? (NOTE: This seemingly proper poem does in fact contain very explicit sexuality.)

EXERCISE 2

Reliability of Dr. Martin Luther King's argument in **"Letter from Birmingham Jail."** The letter contains eight arguments in response to the eight arguments raised by the clergy in their letter of 12 April. The first of these arguments is King's response to the Clergy's claim that he is an "outsider."

HIs evidence for this argument appears primarily in the second and third paragraph of his letter., though later in the essay you may also find material evidence. Evaluate the reliability of King's argument that he is not an outsider.

Alternate Assignment: Evaluate the reliability of ONE of Dr. King's arguments in his powerful anti-Viet Nam sermon, **"A Time to Break Silence,"** delivered on 3 April, 1967, in the pulpit of the Riverside Church in New York City.

EXERCISE 3

See Reliability Evaluation of arguments advanced by Haunani Kay Trask, Hawaiian Separatist and UH Professor, from her book **FROM A NATIVE DAUGHTER.**

UNIT 6: DOCUMENTATION OF THE ESSAY/ GRAMMAR GUIDE

Objectives

To learn to properly document an essay using the Modern Language Association (MLA) Format.

To link to the wonderful Grammar Guide from Webster College.

Discussion

The new MLA documenting convention takes advantage of new technologies, and is quite easy to use. No longer do we have long footnotes or endnotes that contain almost as much material as the old Bibliography entries. Instead we have only two items to master, PARENTHETICAL NOTES and a WORKS CITED list. I think the concepts are easier to understand if we first examine the WORKS CITED list. Before doing that, a brief commercial for a wonderful Grammar Guide:

GRAMMAR GUIDE

At Webster College you can also find a wonderful **GRAMMAR GUIDE**, complete with self- administered quizzes. This site
http://grammar.ccc.commnet.edu/grammar/

will help you with everything from run-on sentences to paragraph and essay organization. Once you have arrived at the guide, select the subject matter that you need the most help with. Download the Powerpoint and name it something that you can find easily. After reading the lesson and viewing the Powerpoint, take the self-administered quizzes. Then move to the next area that you need work on. I would suggest allocating one hour per subject. This is the BEST tool to learn grammar that I know!!

WORKS CITED

WORKS CITED is alphabetical (by author's last name), double-spaced list of the works you have cited to write your paper. This list, and the accompanying parenthetical notes, allow the reader to duplicate your research, or pursue material which she/he finds of interest. The exact (and Works Cited must be exact) format for the entry depends on the type of work you are quoting. Books with one author are cited differently from books with two or more authors. Pamphlets, personal interviews, sacred works are all cited differently and you must refer to a master MLA formatted list.

EASYBIB.COM, a diminutive for "easy bibliography" makes this very easy. See **http://www.easybib.com**

If you want more background go to Palomar College's explanation of how to use Easybib, though I think Easybib is already self-explanatory and very easy to use. The excellent on-line guide at **The MLA Documenting Convention** from Palomar College can be found at http://www2.palomar.edu/pages/library/research-help/citation-style-guides/

AN EXCEPTION TO THE RULE

You will see throughout my samples and student papers, examples in which book titles are in ALL CAPS as opposed to Italics. This is because in the earlier days of the Internet, it was difficult to underline, or italicize. EASYBIB will italicize for you, but I will also accept book titles in ALL CAPS. Note that shorter works, poems, short stories, and articles are shown in quotation marks, NOT italicized or in ALL CAPS. These are works, not separately published which is an easy way to figure out which punctuation to use.

Also, because it is very difficult to indent in email and in html, you need not follow the normal rule for indentation which is to indent six spaces in second and subsequent lines. Again, this is so the author's last name will stand out, making the entries easier to find. I do encourage you to skip a space between WORKS CITED entries.

SECOND, because it is also difficult to underline (italicize) in these two media, I have shown book -length, separately published titles, which would normally be underlined, in ALL CAPS. You may follow that convention for papers submitted electronically in my course. A short story, poem, essay, or work not separately published, should appear in quotation marks, as discussed.

DOCUMENTING ON-LINE SOURCES

EASYBIB.COM is again the gold standard for citing Online sources. The cite for Unit 6 as it is published at De Anza College is

Swensson, John K. "Unit 6 - Documentation of the Essay / Grammar Guide." *Unit 6*. N.p., n.d. Web. 12 Aug. 2016. <https://www.deanza.edu/faculty/swenssonjohn/unit6.html>.
Copy & paste citation What are n.p. & n.d.? | **View in list** | **Edit**

Often you will have no author or publisher known. The key data are Author (if known), Title, URL and the date you visited—which shows how current your research is.

PARENTHETICAL NOTES

are called that because they appear in parentheses and contain only enough data to be clear, usually only the page number, or the author's name and page number. If you were writing a paper about two works by the same author, you might need to add a title to make it clear to which work you were referring. A sample of this is in Unit 4 in the Sample Introductory Para in which the author is clearly using more than one essay by Jeanne Wakatsuki Houston. Indeed when you get to the sample body paragraph of the same theme, you can see the short title of the second essay. You also see some excellent examples of parenthetical notes in Unit 4, "Sample Argumentative Theme #2,

"Why Aren't There More Female Computer Scientists." You use only as much as you need to make the note clear, and you use a note after direct quotations AND summaries: According to Piaget, play, after all, is the way the growing mind gets nourishment (87).

or

Play, after all, is the way the growing mind gets nourishment (Piaget 87). In both of these cases, I can tell that the material comes from an article or book by Piaget, page 87. I need only turn to the Works Cited list at the end of the paper and look alphabetically for the Piaget entry to determine the title and publisher of Piaget's work.

Summary

Documentation is really easy; just follow the guides in Easybib.com

Make sure that your paper contains an exact list, alphabetically by authors last name, of the works you have cited.

The MLA documenting convention for a Works Cited entry for electronic, on-line sources is evolving, but in its simplest form, encompasses four elements, in order:
(1)Author (2)Title of Subpage and Homepage (3)URL (4)Date of YOUR visit. And supplement those Works Cited with simple, Parenthetical Notes that contain the least amount of information necessary to recreate your scholarship.

UNIT 7: STUDENT SUCCESS

Objectives

In all seriousness, the objective of this section is to EMPOWER YOU, the student.

You will learn some tips on Prevailing in College.

You will learn how to begin your decision on selecting a Major that you will enjoy.

You will learn how you can go to any great university, as long as you have a good GPA.

You will be introduced to tools to fund that Education.

You will be introduced to tools that will allow you to write a Resume and find a job.

Discussion

"It's not how good you are, but how BAD you want it!"
Lokelani Yamanoha
Financial Aid Counselor, UH at Maui

This unit, and the accompanying paper on your ten-year life plan (see Unit 7, below; also at Unit 4), are designed to assist you in your quest for success. What is success? To Faulkner it meant prevailing rather than enduring; I think for you that means having choices in your life style. Education, a great education, is what makes those choices possible. So how do you get that great education, pay for it-- better yet get it for free, and enjoy a high quality of life? This section is designed to help you over some of the hurdles, and stimulate your thinking. As John Lennon says, "Imagine," and as Loke says, want it, success, BADLY.

This section is divided into six areas: (1) Self-empowerment in College, (2) Becoming Super Student, (3) Happiness: Aptitude Testing, (4) Picking YOUR best 4 & 6 year Colleges, (5) Marketing yourself: Scholarships & Financial Aid, and (6) Job & Career Plans--Starting Today!

Self-Empowerment in College

College should be a great time in your life; it should be fun, difficult, challenging, rewarding, and energizing. It is a period when you will meet and make new friends who will stay with you throughout your life. In order to empower yourself, take some time to be curious, to discover the many facilities and people at a college who are there to assist you--then make use of their services. Read

through the College Schedule to find out the location of the library with its many electronic assets, the best Computer Center that you can use, the athletic facilities, the security office, and particularly the BIG THREE: the Counseling Center, the Tutorial Center and the Transfer Center. Read through the Student Handbook. Someone took a lot of time to make that publication work for you. Want to get really smart about a college: check the WEB for the College Homepage; it will probably have some neat information that is not contained within print media.

Maui CC Homepage

De Anza CC Homepage

Important Offices on a college campus that can help YOU

ADMISSIONS AND RECORDS

SECURITY OR CAMPUS POLICE

A STARTING POINT

STUDENT ACTIVITIES OFFICE

COUNSELING OFFICE

DISABLED STUDENT SERVICES

DISTANCE LEARNING/ONLINE EDUCATION

EDUCATIONAL DIAGNOSTIC CENTER – for students with Learning Disabilities

EOPS (EXTENDED OPPORTUNITY)

FINANCIAL AID OFFICE

HEALTH OFFICE

STUDENT GOVERNMENT OFFICE

SPECIAL EDUCATION & APPLIED TECHNOLOGIES

TRANSFER/CAREER CENTER

If you are learning disabled or physically challenged, find out what special facilities are available to you. If you are not sure, but think you might need some special assistance, ask a counselor what is available, and/or look for the Special Education Office. Ask a friendly faculty member (there are a few) for assistance.

The key if for YOU to get PROACTIVE and curious, to search out the many, many facilities and people that are available to you. Armando Koghan, one of my best students, once came to my office to ask me to go with him to the cadaver lab (Yes, my college had such a lab), and I did because he was exercising his curiosity--and now pushing mine--. His curiosity made him a great student.

The co-founder of the Jewish Student Union, he transferred to UCLA, but not before teaching me (great students teach teachers) about a facility I had never even known existed on campus.

Becoming Super Student

In the Syllabus, you will find my maxims for student success; I'll repeat them here because they really are the keys to becoming Super Student:

First impressions count.

Master the technology; in order to prevail you must understand Word and Power Point(or equivalent), and how to use email and the Internet. FACEBOOK, TWITTER, INSTAGRAM & YOUTUBE can all help your education. I have not done Twitter yet, but . . . It is OK to be wrong. You learn more when you disagree. Do not be held back by my low standards. Do not be constrained by the Course Assignments; do more than suggested by the course-- again, it is YOUR education. You have a responsibility to your fellow students. The race goes--and college really is competitive-- to those students who get off the mark quickly, and to those students who then discover this secret: helping other students will help you to become a great student yourself. You have to make a lot of choices in college. One of the simpler is what teacher to take for a course. Ask your classmates what their experience has been. If a teacher has a homepage--and many faculty do, you can learn a great deal about the teacher and the course from reviewing the homepage. Or there is always "Rate my Professor," but in any event, do not go into a class flying blind. I am always very impressed by students who ask me questions by email, before the course begins. I pick up Teaching Assistants that way.

Happiness: Aptitude Testing

The choice of a career path is critically important, and one that you can get plenty of good help with, if you will just seek it out. Start by asking yourself a simple question such as "What would I like to major in?" The key word in this question, is "like." Do you like Math better? or English? Which would you rather study? In which subjects do you do well? These questions may lead you to a wise selection of a major. There is an excellent resource at De Anza College called Career Services. This site contains information on a large variety of programs available at the College.

Ordinarily in your first two years you will focus on General Education subjects; that will give you some time to determine which subjects you do like, and to get some help with the important questions about where to continue your studies. Be careful of two traps: doing what your parents think is best for you, or doing what they did, because you know--or think you do--what is involved in THEIR career. Parents usually want the best for their children, but you are old enough to make your own decisions. I have seen many students studying subjects they did not enjoy, just because they were receiving parental pressure to be an Engineer, or go to Berkeley to marry a successful student. I've also seen students start off to be an electrician, because their father was an electrician and wanted them to stay in the family business. The trap here is that you will allow yourself to be steered into an area that is not yours. YOU might as well be happy, and your chance for happiness is greater if you are doing something that you like or are good at. Go to the Career and Transfer

Center and make arrangements to do some Aptitude Testing. EUREKA and SIGI-PLUS are two programs often available.

At UH at Maui, make an appointment at the EOC, Educational Opportunity Center, They make excellent use of the SDS, Holland SELF-DIRECTED SEARCH. this simple test can lead you to a consideration of hundred of occupations that are right for you. There are about a cajillion (a number larger than a google) jobs out there with new ones being invented every day. Today, we all know--at least you should-- what a Web Master is, someone who designs, administers, and manages a WEB site. But twenty one years ago, we did not even have an accessible WEB. An Aptitude Test will help steer you to the field that is right for you, new or traditional.

Picking YOUR best 4 & 6 year Colleges

Once you have determined your aptitudes and major area of interest, you can then begin to think about what college is best for you. I encourage you to dream, think big. You can go anywhere you want. DO NOT EVEN CONSIDER FINANCES. It is not reasonable to say," Well, this life I will go to pretty good school , but next life I will go to a great school." Go to a great school now. We'll see in the next section how to make that happen, how to fund any college. Again the Transfer/ Career Center or the Library is the place to visit.

College libraries often have separate tables with 4 year college information and college catalogues on microfiche, and the reference librarians will be happy to help you. :-)

The Internet has wonderful information about colleges; some colleges will allow you to request applications and more information right off their homepage. On your web browser enter http:// www.collegename.edu and try that for a start. If that does not get you to the college you want, enter the college name in the Yahoo Education Search Engine. I just tried Rice University in Houston, a great school, so wealthy that most students get grants. Rice's Board has told them to get more minority students, to diversify like California. What might be a good school to check out if you are a minority student? I could link their page, but that is too easy. You figure out their address based on the hints given here.

If you want to know which great school is best you for, and visit that school online, you could also start your search at "Princeton Review." This site has listings of the Best Business schools, law schools, medical schools. etc. And you can visit the homepages of virtually every great school in the US here. I highly recommend it.

While you are planning, do not forget your Master's degree, a necessity for most folks of your ilk. A Master's may only take one or two years of residency to acquire, and is a necessity in many professions. Count on taking your Master's at a school different from your undergraduate degree.

Diversity is important to YOUR education. Again, the Libraries/Centers have lists of the best graduate schools within disciplines. Like an Olympic athlete, go for the Gold!

Marketing Yourself: Scholarships and Financial Aid

If you go to a Community College, you get the first two years of your college for very little cost. Therefore you have only two years to fund. Therefore YOU can go to a GREAT school, this life.

If you are going to a great school, do not hesitate to borrow up to $50K for a B.A./B.S., $75K (total for a Master's). You invest in a new car. Sell it, and invest in YOURSELF. This is particularly painless if you qualify for a subsidized Stafford Loan. There are two great on-line assets that

will help you learn about and obtain $ for your education. They are the Financial Aid Information Page and the FASTWEB Scholarship Search. Complete the forms for FASTWEB; it will take you about 15 minutes. 15 minutes later, you will get a prioritized list of the scholarships that FASTWEB's computers believe you are eligible for. You then review each of them, and, if you like, the program will print out a letter request for information. All Free! Want even more information? Enter "Financial Aid" in the Yahoo Education Search Engine, and knock yourself out.

You then have to start writing. You have to write an argument that convinces people that they should fund your education. Schools look for Renaissance people, people who are active in school, in clubs, in the community, students who are multilingual and who have travelled. Schools are often looking for targeted minority students.

The Ten-Year life plan, below is a start to helping you write about yourself. You may also need to ask faculty for letters of recommendation. If you do, give them a resume, or a summary of your life, focusing on your service to school and community, your GPA, your Major, and your family background. Join clubs if you haven't already. The more time a student spends on a campus, the better her/his grades. Clubs and activities help, not hinder, your GPA. Remember Loke's Dictum, It's how bad you want it.

Job & Career Choices--Starting Today!

There are only two kinds of jobs to have in college: those that pay well and those that give you the type of experience you need to achieve your long-term career goal. THERE ARE NO OTHERS!! Fast food is VERBOTEN, unless you wish to run your own restaurant or chain later in your career. (However, my daughter Samantha taught me being a waitress in a high-end restaurant can pay very well.) Jobs that pay well include selling real estate part time (why not make $100K per year, part time, as a student--You do not need a college degree to sell real estate; you only have to take a Community College course in order to pass the State test in CA), WEB Page Designer (Pays about $50 an hour if you do it right). Jobs that prepare you for a career include volunteer in a hospital, if you want to be a doctor; receptionist in a law-firm if you want to be a lawyer.

Otherwise, you should NOT work in college (An exception if you are working on campus, which will probably help your grades.). Sell that car the folks bought for you--a form of indentured servitude, quit your job (unless it meets one of the criteria, above), and become a full -time student. Spend your time in the library becoming SuperStudent, not in McDonald's slinging fries (Cradle-tograve minimum wage at the arches and similar). So how about planning for a real job --if for no other reason than to write the 10 Year Plan below.

There are two really gonzo WEB sites that have lots of great job information. The first, CareerMosaic, also will help you to write a RESUME. The second Monster.com contains everything you ever wanted to know about finding employment. Monster also includes wonderful links to sites with specialized job information.

Summary

Get YOURS!!

Lab

Life. College.

Exercises

EXERCISE 2--TEN YEAR LIFE PLAN-RESEARCH PAPER

"Preparing for the Millenium"

Theme Four is YOUR paper, your MAGNUM OPUS for the course. The PEC incl WORKS CITED, is worth 20 points; the paper itself, will be worth 100 points. Typed, double spaced, the paper's minimum length is 6 pages (2000 words) with 7 references, at least one of which will come from your course readings. There is no maximum length.

It is a personal paper that precisely states your detailed GOAL for the year 20__ (Ten years from NOW!), and ARGUES convincingly how you are going to achieve your goal. The paper will contain three required sections: (Educ=1/2) The EDUCATION PLAN will argue in detail where and when you are going to obtain such education as is necessary to achieve your goal. Why did you choose which college to transfer to? Where and why will you take your graduate work? Where will financing for this education come from? If you decide to take all of your education in the Bay Area (or in Hawaii), defend that geographic choice.

The WORK PLAN will argue in detail where you will work during this period and why. Work would probably support educational financing and career development. How will you get those jobs? In that respect, your GOAL will be stronger if you name a specific type and size of company (or a specific company) rather than just a career field.

The LIFESTYLE PLAN will argue in detail how you will live your life and why. Personal inventory, selection of marital status, alternative lifestyles, and responsibilities toward siblings or parents may enter in here. While this section may require less research, it should be precise and thoughtful. You may include any other sections that you feel you need such as a background section (considering your heredity and environment, a kind of personal asset inventory),real estate or investments, community or religious activities,, service to others, passionate hobbies, sports, etc (or you may wish to include some of these in your LIFESTYLE PLAN.) This is YOUR paper so you

THE TEN YEAR LIFE PLAN: SLIDES

And it's YOUR life. . .

ENVISIONING YOUR Future

- If necessary, do some aptitude testing (EUREKA and DISCOVERY)

- Visit a Counselor

- Think big; you have more potential than you know

- Think specifics: What, where, when, how to get there

- Who can help? Networking. Ask your mentor
- **Do what you like and what you are Excellent at!!!**

- The EDUCATION PLAN will argue in detail where and when you are going to obtain such education as is necessary to achieve your goal. Why did you choose which college to transfer to? Where and why will you take your graduate work? Where will financing for this education come from? If you decide to take all of your education in the Bay Area (or in Hawaii), defend that geographic choice. (1/2 of your paper)

- The WORK PLAN will argue in detail where you will work during this period and why. Work would probably support educational financing and career development. How will you get those jobs? In that respect, your GOAL will be stronger if you name a specific type and size of company (or a specific company) rather than just a career field.

- The LIFESTYLE PLAN will argue in detail how you will live your life and why. Personal inventory, selection of marital status, alternative lifestyles, and responsibilities toward siblings or parents, hobbies, and/or interests may enter in here. While this section may require less research, it should be precise and thoughtful.

- OVERVIEW: You may include any other sections that you feel you need such as a background section (considering your heredity and environment, a kind of personal asset inventory), real estate or investments, community or religious activities, service to others, passionate hobbies, sports, etc. (or you may wish to include some of these in your LIFESTYLE PLAN.) This is YOUR paper so you have free reign. You may write in the future tense or the past tense--just be consistent and remember that this is argument, NOT FANTASY. Your choices will be tested for the quality of research and rationality within the context of the choice. If you choose mediocrity, you must defend that choice.

Your Education Plan

- The EDUCATION PLAN will argue in detail where and when you are going to obtain such education as is necessary to achieve your goal. Why did you choose which college to transfer to? Where and why will you take your graduate work? Where will financing for this education come from? If you decide to take all of your education in the Bay Area (or in Hawaii), defend that geographic choice. (1/2 of your paper)

- Go to some great school in YOUR field

- Private schools may be less expensive

- Get out of CA if you grew up here

- Interview 4 year reps and graduates of the school you select (Do a Transfer Admission Agree mentas backup)

- Interview Financial Aid staff to determine financing

- Go to http://www.fastweb.com for scholarships

- Visit TRANSFER CENTER for help

- Do WEB Search of schools and VISIT your choice.

- Consider alternate funding sources: church/temple/mosque, work, military.

- Include Masters Degree in most cases

- See a Counselor here to schedule transfer and Graduation

YOUR Work Plan

- The WORK PLAN will argue in detail where you will work during this period and why. Work would probably support educational financing and career development. How will you get those jobs? In that respect, your GOAL will be stronger if you name a specific type and size of company (or a specific company) rather than just a career field.

- Do a Resume and Cover Letter for your Mentor

- Only Two Kinds of Jobs: Related to Ten Year goal (Internships?) or $$$$$

- Consider Scholarships, loans or Grants vice work--the three year graduation by working hard

- Big Company or Small Company and in what order?

- Interview your Mentor

YOUR LIFESTYLE PLAN

- The LIFESTYLE PLAN will argue in detail how you will live your life and why. Personal inventory, selection of marital status, alternative lifestyles, and responsibilities toward siblings or parents, hobbies, and/or interests, may enter in here. While this section may require less research, it should be precise and thoughtful.

- Yes, you can "plan" how to find the right partner

- Family can limit or enhance--up to you

- Hobbies important. What do you LOVE to do? And where?

- Why not Hawaii? Think outside the box.

- Your plan-not your parents!!!!

- Community Service Important!!

The Logic of this Plan. . .

- You may include any other sections that you feel you need such as a background section (considering your heredity and environment, a kind of personal asset inventory),real estate or investments, community or religious activities, service to others, passionate hobbies, sports, etc. (or you may wish to include some of these in your LIFESTYLE PLAN.) This is YOUR paper so you have free reign. You may write in the future tense or the past tense--just be consistent and remember that this is argument, NOT FANTASY. Your choices will be tested for the quality of research and rationality within the context of the choice. If you choose mediocrity, you must defend that choice.
- **You are arguing a thesis: If I follow this plan, I can achieve MY specific, stated goal.**
- OK to be a "Fish Crier" ala Carl Sandburg, but your plan will argue how you can be the best fish crier, and have the ability to make choices.

UNIT 8: CULTURAL CONSIDERATIONS

Objectives

To prevail in the third millenium by learning about different cultures.

To investigate stereotypes and racism.

Discussion

Why is a male student wearing a dress in my class?

A key component of prevailing in the future is to understand and appreciate different cultures. This is so because of the polyglot world in which we live, and technology is making it ever smaller, throwing us closer together. In California, whites are the new minority, and we have a very large immigrant and foreign population. One of the strengths of De Anza College is that over 45% of our students are Asian. In Hawaii, differing cultures have coexisted for a long time with at least the veneer of tranquility. Though what about Haoles vs. Locals? (Haole is a Hawaiian pejorative term for white people meaning "without soul.")

Since we are about prevailing rather than enduring, it is appropriate that we examine different cultures as a part of all of our courses, and there is no better place than to start with ourselves, the members of the multicultural learning community in the classroom. In my Freshman Composition classes we often start with the formal (or informal depending on the culture) Cultural Reports found in Exercise 1, below.

In other courses we will examine the literature of different cultures. What similarities are there between Shakespeare's HAMLET and Mishima's "Patriotism," the story of two ultranationalist lovers in Japan? What can Asian (and other) students learn from Wallace Steven's great "Peter Quince at the Clavier," set in a Shakespearean play, but using Christian Biblical images from the OLD TESTAMENT? What lessons about haves and have nots do we learn from the most important recent novel published,

THE KITE RUNNER?

In class one year students were acting "Peter Quince." Now we understand why the student--who shall remain nameless for obvious reasons is wearing a dress. He was acting out the line "thinking of your blue shadowed silk is music." ☺

What does Li Po's (pronounced Li Bao) 7th century poem "The River Merchant's Wife," say to Hispanic or Eritrean or Ethiopian students?

Or Honkies?--a word that originally was a derogatory word for Hungarian immigrants to the US.

After we have a sufficient trust established, we will be fairly direct (in your face) about these discussions, but we must remember the cardinal rule not to offend. Why do we laugh at ethnic humor such as that found at the start of BLAZING SADDLES? What fears are associated with stereotypes? Is it true most Asians are slow drivers? How about Deadheads? What kinds of "in groups" and "out groups" are you a part of, and how do you excel in a multicultural, potentially confusing environment? What are the roles of language in that environment, and what language(s) should we speak?

In many classes we examine multicultural essays or literature. In English 1A we sometimes read Louise Erdrich's novel LOVE MEDICINE about the Catholic Church's administering, on behalf of the US government, a Native American reservation, to the point of supplanting the Indian gods with their Christian god? What happens to one's identity when that happens? We often read Robert Olen Butler's great (Pulitzer Prize, 1993) short story "Mr. Green," about a Viet Namese woman who has the soul of her Grandfather in her parrot (see Exercise 2); what happens to your identity when there are competing religions within the family, and the family keeps getting refugeed, fleeing from Hanoi in 54, Saigon in 75? We also often read Jeanne Wakatsuki Houston's great memoir, FAREWELL TO MANZANAR (coauthored with her late husband James Houston) about what it was like to grow up in the Internment camps during WWII, when, for fear of the Japanese, our government imprisoned most Japanese-Americans.

Jeanne Houston's essays "Beyond Manzanar; An examination of Asian-American Womanhood," and "A Tapestry of Hope," an original piece first delivered as the graduation address to the De Anza Graduating Class of 1994, (See Unit Two of this text,) speaks to us of positive coexistence in very insightful ways, no matter what our ethnic persuasion or beliefs.

In the Summer of 1995, I had thirty students in my class from the US, Viet Nam, China, and Eritrea. 12 of these students transferred to UC Davis!
Sample Paper

The Asian Experience by Inoh H.

When I first read the play THE SOUND OF A VOICE, I felt a strong sense of connection with the two characters in the play. In a way, it made me more aware of my own cultural background as an Asian-American. Therefore I felt that it is more meaningful for me to research this play. I have come across several different articles which helped me to appreciate the play a little bit better. The first article was a biography of David Henry Hwang. In the biography Hwang mentioned that when he was younger, he regarded his Chinese ancestry as a minor detail, sort of like having red hair" (Hwang). Being an Asian American, I can identify with what he is saying. I grew up in the mid - west, and I can honestly say that people in that part of world are not very kind to foreigners. The ignorance of some people in this country really frustrates me. And the second article was a review of the movie THE JOY LUCK CLUB by Roger Ebert. The review mentioned that "Women were not valued very highly" (Ebert). Those with independent minds and spirits were valued even less than the docile, obedient ones; this reflected how Hwang portrayed the Woman in THE SOUND OF A VOICE. Ebert's view is also an important trait of the Asian culture. So I have decided on my theme. The writer, David Henry Hwang, has contributed a great deal to the Asian American community with his play THE SOUND OF A VOICE I say this because he is allowing the younger generations of Asian Americans to be more aware of the significance of their own heritage and to distinguish the differences between the Eastern and the Western cultures. Most Asian Americans who grew up in America as children often resent their ethnicity because of racism and criticism they have encountered regarding their race.

The play THE SOUND OF A VOICE is socially significant because it allows the audience a glimpse of the Asian culture through human interactions. The proper etiquette of the Eastern culture is somewhat different from the Western culture; the way we respond to certain things in America would be considered inappropriate and sometimes even rude in the East. In the JOY LUCK CLUB movie we hear: "Waverly: But the worst is when Rich criticizes my mother's cooking, and he didn't even know what he had done. As is the Chinese cook's custom, my mother always insults her own cooking, but only with the dishes she served with special pride. Lindo: This dish not salty enough, no flavor, it's too bad to eat. Please. Waverly: That was our cue to eat some and proclaim it the best she ever made. At this point Rich takes a bite and says 'All it needs is some soy sauce. And he proceeds to drown it with soy sauce.'" (Tan 46:30) This might be one struggle that Asian Americans might encounter in their everyday lives. In schools and out in society they are taught one set of rules for interacting with one another, and at home they are taught another set of rules. Some of them might arrive at the conclusion that what they learn in society and everyday life is the right way and what the parents are trying to force upon them is the wrong way. No one has told them that there are different rules to the game of life and that they should learn to distinguish between the two of them. This might be the reason why there is a lot of culture clash between different groups. Through the play THE SOUND OF A VOICE we will be able to distinguish the significance of the traits within the Eastern culture from that of the Western culture.

In scene one of THE SOUND OF A VOICE we get a sense of how Asian women behave. First we see that when the Woman was serving some tea to the Man, she had a hard time accepting any compliment, "M: The tea- you pour it well, W: no, M: the sound it makes-in the cup-very soothing. W: that's the tea's skill, not mine"(Hwang 1199). She makes it seem like it is a crime to accept any praises for her services, but actually it's an act of being humble. If this situation were to take place in America, the Woman would have just say "Thank you," and move on. Next, we see that there are two significant traits being displayed. The first trait we see is when the Woman was offering the Man some food, the Man kept refusing: "W: May I get you something else? Rice, perhaps? M: No, W: And some vegetables? M: No, thank you. W: Fish? It is at least two days walk to the nearest village. I saw no horse. You must be very hungry. You would do great honor to dine with me. Guests are rare. M: Thank you" (Hwang 1199). From this scene we see that when the Man was offered food, he kept refusing until the Woman insisted for the third time. It seems that it is impolite to accept anything on the first try. And the other trait, which was displayed, was the fact that the Woman kept offering her guest something to eat even after her guest had refused the offer. The way these two characters interact with each other seems like a ritual. This particular trait displayed by the Woman is something you don't see westerners do at all. This is an Eastern trait because in America the host will offer something once, and if the guest refuses, they will allow the guest to help themselves whenever they like. The movie THE JOY LUCK CLUB also portrays this type of behavior. There was one scene in the movie where the hostess brought out some food from the kitchen and proceeded to pack the guest's plate full of food. "June: Oh, oh, thank you, OK, OK, OK, enough. Aunty Lindo: What is the matter guest of honor, you should eat more. You are getting too skinny" (Tan 52:23) We can see that the guest did not want any more food, but Aunty Lindo kept insisting that she take more.

And also in the play THE SOUND OF A VOICE the author David Henry Hwang, portrays a man who appears to be an old Samurai and a woman who was supposed to be a witch. The significance of the male character in the play is pretty important because when we hear the word "Samurai," what comes to my mind are honor, loyalty, discipline, bravery, and justice. They are the best swordsmen in the land, and whoever can control them pretty much controls the land. I believe David Henry Hwang was using the traits of the Samurai to represent the Asian culture and what we stand for. He wanted Asian Americans to know that we do have something to be proud of.

The primary trait of the Samurai is honor. Throughout our lives as students we usually associate the word "honor" with "class" (honor class) or "roll" (honor roll). And the older generation might associate the word "honor" with Honor Blackman as Pussy Galore in the James Bond movie GOLDFINGER. We try to please our parents any way possible without giving any thought as to what it really means. Rule number one by Miyamoto Musashi is "Think of what is right and true," (16) tells us that to be honorable we should do the right thing. The Man in the play did what is right and true by not lying to her: "M: If I gave you a name it would only be made up; why should I deceive you. You are too kind for that" (Hwang 1201). And he also showed that he was true to his word, when he was practicing his skills, by resting his chin on the tip of the sword: "M: Come any closer and Iّll drop my head"(Hwang 1211) The book mentioned that after she went closer and grabbed the sword, the man reached up to his chin and felt a drop of blood. This also proves that he was true to his word because when she went closer he actually applied pressure toward the sword and therefore cut himself.

The other honorable thing the Man did was when the Man tried to leave in the middle of the night. From the play we know that the man's intention from the beginning was to kill the woman because she was a witch, "W: Yes I have heard of them. From other visitors-young-hotblooded-or old- who came here because they were told great glory was to be had by killing the witch in the woods. M: I was told that no one could spend time in this house without falling in love" (Hwang 1209) He has so much pride that he has to sneak out at night without telling her. What he tried to do might not fit the traditional meaning of being honorable, but he did it because to harm someone he had befriended was considered to be dishonorable.

Another thing we can learn from the play is to look at the two characters and see what they represent. We can picture the Man as a symbol of all the Asian immigrants who are in this country, and the Woman as representing the United States of America as a metaphor. She symbolizes the land of opportunity. She cares for the flowers, and they represent the beauty and prosperity of this country. In Chinese, the words that are used to name America translate into "beautiful country." But when the Asian immigrants arrive in this country, they see that it is not as people say. Things are tougher than people say they are. They face many difficulties from society. It is also next to impossible to leave when they wanted to because they have sacrificed almost everything to be here, and now they have nothing to go back to, almost too ashamed to crawl back to friends and families to ask for help. At the end we see the Man pick up the flute and play it. The flute symbolizes the hard work it takes to make it in this country because during the play the Woman played the flute for the flowers to keep them staying fresh and beautiful. So in order to continue the beauty, he starts playing the Shakuhachi.

I believe that through his efforts, David Henry Hwang, has contributed a great deal to the Asian American community with his play THE SOUND OF A VOICE. He is preserving our heritage for the younger generations of Asian Americans to be more aware of the significance of their own heritage and to distinguish the differences between the Eastern and the Western cultures.

Works Cited

"Biography of David Henry Hwang," http://occ.awlonline.com/bookbind/pubbooks/ kennedycompact_awl/chapter2 6/deluxe.html (21 Jun. 2000)

Hwang, David Henry. "The Sound of A Voice." Literature: An Introduction to Fiction, Poetry, and Drama. Ed. X.J. Kennedy and Dana Gioia. 2nd Compact ed. New York: Longman, 2000. 1199-1213.

Ebert, Roger. Movie review of the movie "The Joy Luck Club." http://www.suntimes.com/ebert/ebert_reviews/1993/09/878918.html (18 Jun .2000)

Musashi, Miyamoto. THE BOOK OF FIVE RINGS. New York: Barnes & Noble, 1997.

Exercises

CULTURAL REPORTS

This assignment is intended to be accomplished in groups of 2-4 students. With my prior approval a student may give a solo presentation if she/he is a member of a culture not represented by others, i.e. if Chidi Obi is not a member of a cultural group such as Deadheads or Hell's Angels or similar, she may report on her home culture in Nigeria.

YOU ARE THE TEACHERS. Your group must decide what you wish to teach the class about your cultural group. What defines your culture; what characterizes your society? If your group is one of persons who come from another part of the world, what should we know about your home country? Geography? Religions? Languages? Costumes? Food (pls do not bring any)?

As part of your research for this presentation, put your group into Yahoo or some other search engine, i.e. "Hispanic Culture," "Philippine Culture," African-American Culture." You will be amazed at the treasure of cultural information available.

What can you tell us about the history of your group's migrations to this country? Are there stereotypes (generalizations-see Unit 5) associated with your group that are correct? Incorrect?

We would like to hear from each member of your group; each presenter will be graded separately, although a strong team effort will undoubtedly help everyone. Please coordinate all handouts (Do not forget Power Point), videos, WEB presentations, and other audiovisual requirements in advance.

Presentations will be scheduled one week in advance. Each presentation will last between ten and twenty minutes, and we will have no more than three per day. Your group MUST get together outside of class for your REHEARSAL.

UNIT 9: EDITING SKILLS

Objectives

To learn Revision and Editing Skills.

To learn how to proofread.

To learn what happens when a Peer Editing Copy (PEC) is due.

To learn some basic Correction Symbols primarily so that you might understand my comments, and secondarily so that you might be able to use them to edit each other's work.

Discussion

Editing papers is a critical skill, not just for me so that I may draw my meager paycheck, but FOR YOU, so that you may learn good writing by editing the work of your peers. Recall two points from the Syllabus. First: In Collaborative Learning, we learn the things that we teach. Therefore, if you teach your fellow classmate what needs to be improved in her paper, you will learn by teaching. Second, recall that not only is your editing graded, but that days when Peer Editing Copies (PECs) are due are the most critical days in the course. On those days, a lot of learning takes place as you edit your peer's work, and they edit yours. Not only is your PEC draft graded, but your editing that you do on that day will also be graded. Do not choose a PEC day to go to the beach in Santa Cruz, or Kihei.

Revision and Editing Skills

With your own draft at hand (which is the end product of much brainstorming and organizing according to the principles of argumentation in Units 3,4 and 5 which resulted in a great draft with scintillating specific, concrete, and convincing evidence,) underline your thesis with two lines, and your topic sentences with one line.

Look at each of them to determine whether they are Restricted, Unified, and Precise (RUP). Do the words "I say this because" appear immediately after your thesis, followed by your Plan Step which is the summary of your topic sentences--your underlining should assist in this evaluation. Look at each body paragraph and apply the UOCC test-Is the paragraph Unified, Ordered, Complete, and Coherent? Review Unit 3 if you have questions about this. After you have revised and now have another draft, edit your own paper. After editing, you now have a third draft--this is easier than it sounds since you are doing all of this on a computer.

Now it is time to PROOFREAD! Do a computerized spellcheck. Also do a computerized grammar check (Windows 6.0 and later). The grammar check is correct approximately 50% of the time and wrong 50% of the time. But it affords you the opportunity to think critically 100% of the time.

After you do these two computerized steps, it will STILL be necessary to proofread, because the computer cannot normally understand the context of a word. Recently a student sent me a request for a letter, saying there was a "death line," rather than a "deadline." A super student (3.96 GPA), but he failed to proofread. Would he have a 4.0 if he had exhibited better proofreading skills?
Special Note for ESL Writers.

Proofreading is particularly critical for ESL students, because not only is English a foreign language for you, but your own language is structured with different rules. Since you probably speak better than you write, one trick is to turn the written word into speech. In a quiet place listen to yourself reading YOUR OWN paper ALOUD. If you hear something you suspect is wrong, it probably is-if you feel some tension in your face, or pause momentarily, you probably have an error.

Also try reading each word aloud, backwards; this may help you to determine word omissions. Yes, I know there are no verb tenses in Chinese and no articles-that's why this test is so good. Thanks.
Peer Editing

Your very important assignment on a PEC (Peer Editing Copy) day is to bring to class a typed, complete, double spaced paragraph or theme, depending on the assignment. You may bring this on disc-if it's compatible, and you had best determine that before coming to the lab-or on paper.

I will give you two copies of the PEC sheet which is normally yellow in color--depending on what color the trees were. You will complete the sheet on two of your classmates' papers, and will have your paper edited by two of your classmates.

Editing consists of completing the PEC sheet and marking on the draft.

You then take home your marked up draft which will have comments in two different handwritings, and two yellow sheets. You will then revise, and then PROOFREAD again. (You may even wish to ask a classmate to reedit your "final" paper.) When the final paper is due, you will turn in your final copy, the two yellow sheets, and the original PEC. It is at that point, I will grade your paper, and the editing.

On PEC day, I will come around and "weigh" your paper, i.e. do the quantitative assessment. Is it all there? Typed, double spaced? Complete? That is about all I will have time for. You and your classmates will perform the qualitative assessment.

Nice persons finish last. Be critical. Be tough-for that will help your classmate. If Sally's paper is weak, and you say, "looks good to me," it will not help Sally--and your editing grade will not look very good to you.

Note: Before you give your paper to your classmate for editing you should have already done the Spelling and Grammar checks. Do not waste your classmates' time, by giving her/him an un-proofed paper. We may do machine editing vice using the yellow sheets. I will show you how to do that using the Insert Annotation feature on Word 6.0 or later. If your dog ate your disc on PEC day, he will also have eaten your grade.

There are no makeups except for family emergencies, coordinated in advance. If you have brain surgery scheduled for PEC day, at least make sure your paper gets to class, even if you do not. PECs are generally worth 20% of your entire grade, and their quality is often the difference between A's and B's, B's and C's, etc.

For Online classes, I require every paper after the first to be peer edited by a minimum of one classmate, and I require, conversely, every student to peer edit one paper. When you submit your paper, you will list the name of your editor in your Works Cited. If your paper is weak, the editor owns that, and I will note that. I also encourage you to take your paper to AT 309 (The Writing Center) or get online tutoring help and to note that in your Works Cited. I am impressed with students who take the time to go by AT 309, and your efforts will be noted.
Correction Symbols:

Listed below in alphabetical order are the explanations of the hieroglyphics you will find on your papers. You are also encouraged to consult a writing handbook, or the WRITERS GUIDE which is a link on my homepage. I encourage YOU to use these symbols when you are peer editing your classmate's work. They are fairly standard.

SYMBOL followed by EXPLANATION

//ism Parallelism needed
AGR Subject-Verb Agreement
AWK Awkward Phraseology
CAP Capitalization Error
CONTR Too informal to use Contractions in a College Writing Class
CW Word Choice is poor
do Ditto-Same Mistake Again
ESL A problem caused by lack of familiarity with English
FRAG Sentence Fragment
GR Grammar Error
HW Handwriting or Printer Problem--get a new cartridge
LOG Logic Error--See Unit 5
M Inadequate or Wrong Size Margin
MM Misplaced Modifier
P Punctuation Error, See Writers Guide in Unit 6
PAS Passive Voice
Para or PP No new paragraph, or needs new paragraph
RA Read Aloud and Correct--Often helps ESL students

REF Pronoun Referent
REP Repetitious
RS Run-on Sentence

RTP	Read The Problem--You did not follow instructions
S or SP	Spelling Error---Use the Spellcheck
SH	Improper shift in voice or tense
SPT	Inadequate Support for argument in Evidence or Analysis–Review Unit 3
TRANS	A transition is weak or absent
TS	Error in Topic Sentence- should be an opinion-not fact See Unit 3
U	Unity Error
VT	Verb Tense is Incorrect
WD	Wordy, flowery *tagalog*-like sentence ☺
SMP	SEE ME PLEASE---or call 408-590-4430, or email

Sample Peer Edited Essay

This is the original, unedited version, followed by the peer edited version.

BLIND BY FAITH

Is it possible for a man to be so hypnotized by faith that he is incapable of apprehending the truth that surrounds him? Yes. The principle of faith centers heavily around the confident belief of an idea set by an individual or community. The story takes place during the period when all devoted Puritans adopt Calvinism; Goodman Brown being one of them. Calvinism presents the idea that all men are born sinful because of Original Sin. That is, all men are essentially evil within. Moreover, it preaches once man has sinned, he is "incapable of any spiritual good" (Hanko 2). Goodman Brown himself is a Puritan, but he is unable to see the dark side of human nature that runs parallel to the faith of his community. The faith in which he only sees the good in mankind is unique to him, thus resulting in the rejection of reality. "We are a people of prayer, and good works, to boot, and abide no such wickedness" (198), he says. The conflict between Goodman Brown's faith and that set by the community is apparent in the story. Hawthorne uses the imagery of nature to develop the theme of appearance versus reality. I say this because the path in the forest symbolically plays a role in exposing the reality that Goodman Brown rejects. He goes in the forest and walks along the path as a deceived man and exits with a shocking new view. Another use of nature is the serpent, which is a representation of Goodman Brown's deceived life.

The path in the forest represents Goodman Brown's foreshadowing perception of human nature as evil. The path through the dark woods depicts his naive view of mankind as "angelic." Filled with "innumerable trunks and thick boughs" (197), the path represents a giant wall of obscurity that has been shoved in front of Brown's face for his entire life. Feeling his way through the dark wilderness and anticipating the evil that is lurking ahead, Brown is like an innocent student yearning for knowledge. In this case, knowledge is facing the fact that "evil is the nature of mankind" (205). Furthermore, along the path the mysterious traveler "[plucks] a branch of maple and [begins] to strip it of the twigs and little boughs" for a walking stick that was later given to Brown (200). The stripping of the branch signifies the "stripping" of Brown's faith, thus foretelling his inevitable yield to reality. Another way nature plays a role in pulling down the curtain of deception is the fact that the path is narrow at the beginning of the journey and then comes to a clearing at the end. This is indicative of Brown's pure, but narrow-minded perception of the good in human nature. However, as the path widens his faith begins to diminish and his views become more open. In the end, he finally succumbs to reality, and the reality is that all humans are sinners.

Likewise, the imagery of the serpent can be interpreted as a representation of deception. Of great significance to the story, the serpent-like staff carried by the mysterious figure personifies Goodman Brown's misconceptions of the unknown in human nature. Brown has been deceived by a highly programmed society to believe that humans are virtuous, but he comes to realize that when the curtain is pulled down, their evil nature manifests. The serpent is a suitable representation for deceit as they can appear one way, then shed their skins and appear differently. According to THE OLD TESTAMENT, it was the serpent that tricked Adam and Eve into eating the forbidden apples. "And the LORD God said unto the woman, What is this that thou hast done? And the woman said, The serpent beguiled me, and I did eat" (Genesis 3:13). Even in nature, the serpent is seen as a cunning creature. The serpent, such as the cobra, is able to spread the hood around the area of its head and neck to make it appear larger to its prey and predators. Ironically, in the story it is the serpent staff that divulges the falsification of Goody Cloyse. With his serpent staff, the mysterious traveler "[touches] her withered neck with what seemed the serpent's tail" (199). Consequently, the "pious old lady" reveals herself as a witch and a friend of the Devil. As soon as Goodman Brown sees his community participating in the satanic act, and himself inevitability succumbing to evil, the serpent staff is not spoken of again.

The path in the forest, along with the imagery of the serpent associated with the mysterious traveler's staff, are symbolic of a mind that has been misguided by his misleading faith. As his allegorical name implies, the virtuous nature of Goodman Brown deters him from seeing his community in a different light. His faith conflicts with the faith of his community. The devotion to his faith causes him to live a life of obscurity and results in a detrimental yield to reality. In the end, he is constantly reminded of the evil that he had witnessed in the forest as he rejects everyone in his community. The use of nature by Hawthorne demonstrates the conflict between the world of fantasy versus the cruel nature of reality. The fantasy in the story is the faith of a sinless society; however, the reality is that sin is a part of human nature, which parallels the beliefs of Calvinism.

WORKS CITED

Hanko, Herman. "The Five Points of Calvinism." 1976: Internet. < http://www.prca.org/ five-points/chapter1.html> 29 January 2000.

Hawthorne, Nathaniel. "Young Goodman Brown." LITERATURE: AN INTRODUCTION TO FICTION, POETRY, AND DRAMA. Eds. X.J. Kennedy and Dana Gioia. 7th ed. New York: Longman, 1999. 196-206.

L, Nakyeong. Peer Editor. Cyber-classmate to the author of this paper. 3 Feb. 2000: 2 hours.

L, Dazhi. Peer Editor. Cyber-classmate to the author of this paper. 3 Feb. 2000: 45 minutes.

The Old Testament: King James Version. "Genesis." Chapter 3, Verse 13. 1997: Internet.< http://www.weblicity.com/freedom/bible/GE_idx.html> 27 Jan. 2000.

BLIND BY FAITH
Edited by Nakyeong L.
(Student editor comments in ALL CAPS)

Is it possible for a man to be SO hypnotized by faith that he is incapable of apprehending the truth that surrounds him? Yes. The principle of faith centers heavily around the confident belief of an idea set by a person or community. In Nathaniel Hawthorne's "Young Goodman Brown," the faith of an individual conflicts with the faith of the community. The story takes place during the period where all devoted Puritans adopt Calvinism; Goodman Brown being one of them. Calvinism presents the idea that all men are born sinful because of Original Sin. That is, all men are essentially evil within. Moreover, it preaches once man has sin, he is "incapable of any spiritual good" (Hanko 2). Goodman Brown himself is a Puritan, but he is unable to see the dark side of human nature that runs parallel to the faith of his community. The faith that he has is unique to him, thus resulting in the rejection of reality. I FEEL IT IS A LITTLE BIT SUDDEN HERE WHEN YOU TURN TO THE THESIS FROM THE DISCUSSION ABOVE. MAYBE USE A TRANSITION? In the story, Hawthorne uses the imagery of nature to develop the theme of appearance vs. reality. MR.SWENSSON SAID NOT TO START WITH THE WORDS "IN THE STORY" OR "I BELIEVE" BECAUSE THAT WOULD BE WORDY. I say this because the forest plays a role in exposing the reality that Goodman Brown rejects. He went in a deceived man and exits with a shocking new view. Another use of nature is the serpent, which is quite an appropriate symbol for deception.

The forest INSTEAD OF FOREST, SPECIFY THE SUBJECT LIKE PATH represents Goodman Brown's foreshadowing perception of human nature as evil. The path through the dark woods is itself symbolic of his naive perception of human beings as "angelic." Filled with "innumerable trunks and thick boughs" (HAWTHORNE -GIVE AN AUTHOR'S LAST NAME 197), the path suggests the obscure and misleading views WHAT ARE HIS VIEWS? Brown has on mankind. Feeling his way through the dark wilderness and anticipating the evil that is lurking ahead, Brown is like an innocent student yearning for knowledge. In this case, knowledge is facing the fact that "evil is the nature of mankind" (HAWTHORNE 205), as the mysterious traveler puts it. During the journey, the dark figure "[plucks] a branch of maple and [begins] to strip it of the twigs and little boughs" for a walking stick that was later given to Brown (200). The stripping of the branch signifies the "stripping" of Brown's faith DEAL WITH ONLY PATH-FOCUS ON ONE SUBJECT, thus foretelling his inevitable yield to reality. Another way nature plays a role in pulling down the curtain of deception is the fact that the path is narrow at the beginning of the journey and then comes to a clearing at the end. This is indicative of Brown's pure, but narrow-minded perception of the good in human nature. However, as the path widens his faith begins to diminish and his views become more open. In the end, he finally succumbs to reality, and the reality is that all humans are sinners.

Likewise, the imagery of the serpent can be interpreted as a representation of deception. Of great significance to the story, the serpent-like staff carried by the mysterious figure personifies Goodman Brown's misconceptions of the unknown in human nature. Brown has been deceived by a highly programmed society to believe that humans are virtuous, but he comes to realize that when the curtain is pulled down, their evil nature manifests. The serpent is a suitable representation for deceit as they can appear one way, then shed their skins and appear differently. According to THE

OLD TESTAMENT, it was the serpent that tricked Adam and Eve into eating the forbidden apples; "Then the LORD God said to the woman, "what is this that you have done?" The woman said, "The serpent beguiled me, and I ate" (Genesis 3:13). Even in nature, the serpent is seen as a cunning creature. The serpent, such as the cobra, is able to spread the hood around the area of its head and neck to make it appear larger to its prey and predators. Ironically, in the story it is the serpent staff that divulges the falsification of Goody Cloyse. With his serpent staff, the mysterious traveler "[touches] her withered neck with what seemed the serpent's tail" (HAWTHORNE 199). Consequently, the "pious old lady" reveals herself as a witch and a friend of the devil. As soon as Goodman Brown sees his community participating in the satanic act, and himself inevitability succumbing to evil, the serpent staff is not heard of again.

The trees and brushes NOT PATH? in the forest, along with the imagery of the serpent associated with the mysterious traveler's staff, are symbolic of a mind that is just about to be exposed to reality. As his allegory ALLEGORICAL name implies, the virtuous nature of Goodman Brown deters him from seeing his community in a different light. His devotion to his own faith results in a detrimental yield to reality. In the end, he himself becomes evil HE DOESN'T BECOME EVIL. HE JUST AVOIDS THE EVIL. as he rejects everyone in his community. The use of nature by Hawthorne demonstrates the conflict between the world of fantasy versus the cruel nature of reality. The fantasy in the story is the faith of a sinless society; however, the reality is that sin is a part of human nature, which parallels the beliefs of Calvinism.

PRETTY GOOD PAPER . I PARTICULARLY LIKE THE FACT THAT YOUR PLAN STEP IS SO CLEAR. GOOD LUCK--Nakyeong

Summary

You will learn by editing, and
The Race goes to she who cares enough to proofread well.

UNIT 10: ANALYZING AND WRITING ABOUT LITERATURE

Some Literature and Composition Links (to warm up):

Or how to enjoy some of the great literature of the world, and learn Composition skills, without buying more textbooks!

Vanderbilt's Internet Literature Resources

Links to English Departments, General Literature Indexes, Electronic Text Archives including all of Shakespeare, and much more!

OLEMISS- The Literature of William Faulkner

UCONN- Bleiler's List of Great Books

This is an amazing list. Do not miss the OXFORD ENGLISH DICTIONARY, the link to UCSB's "Voice of the Shuttle," and the link to UVA's Electronic Texts.

Sentence Animation Demonstration

Objectives

To learn strategies to facilitate our understanding of literature.

To understand a methodology for evaluating Prose.

To understand a strategy for understanding Poetry.

To begin to learn how to write effectively about literature.

Discussion

ANALYZING & WRITING ABOUT LITERATURE

"I mind I used to think that hope was all man had, and then I realized that was all he needed-jest hope."

William Faulkner

English for Argumentative Writing

What follows is a mere overview, an attempt to consolidate terminology and a general approach which will allow us all to work better together, with a common vocabulary and understanding. This handout should be supplemented with, at minimum, the study of Chapter 37 in LITERATURE: AN INTRODUCTION TO FICTION, POETRY, AND DRAMA (LIT), "Writing about Literature" (1393). All parenthetical page references that follow are to LIT (Second Compact Edition).

If you are using Kennedy & Gioia's anthology, LITERATURE: AN INTRODUCTION TO FICTION,POETRY, AND DRAMA (LIT), the normal EWRT 1B text, look up the terms in the index in the back of the book. Also scan the table of Contents in the front of the text. You will note that there is an entire section in the back of this text called "Writing" (LIT 1391-1499). It is worth the price of the text by itself.

All literature may be better appreciated from the title of the late John Ciardi's great critical work, HOW DOES A POEM MEAN? If we analyze a poem, a short story, a novel, or a play or movie from the perspective of its component parts, we can "put it back together again" with a better understanding of HOW it works. Not only will you understand the work better, you will be able to more clearly articulate your own evaluation of the effectiveness of the work and the techniques that underly the effectiveness.

We shall examine how THEMES, or major ideas of the author are developed by her using

1. PLOT or STRUCTURE

2. SETTING

3. IMAGERY or DICTION

4. CHARACTER AND CHARACTERIZATION and

5. POINT OF VIEW

THEMES are major ideas that are contained WITHIN a work. Themes are different from MEANING-which is YOUR OWN personal response to the literature.
A VARIANT FOR POETRY—the John Ciardi model

Typically, we shall examine POETRY from the three-headed vision of IMAGERY, SOUND, and STRUCTURE. But we supplement this by asking the questions 1. "Who is the speaker?" which carries implications about CHARACTER and POINT OF VIEW and 2.

"What is the occasion?" which carries implications about SETTING and CHARACTER. SOUND is typically of greater import in poetry than prose, and may contribute to themes.

The British poet, Henry Reed, has written a poem, "Naming of Parts," which is ideal for examining how contrasts in each of the three elements, IMAGERY, SOUND, and STRUCTURE, contributes to the author's THEME. Ask yourself the two questions "Who is the Speaker" and "What is the Occasion," and READ THIS POEM ALOUD:

Unit 10

NAMING OF PARTS by Henry Reed

To-day we have naming of parts. Yesterday,
We had daily cleaning. And to-morrow morning,
We shall have what to do after firing. But to-day,
To-day we have naming of parts. Japonica
Glistens like coral in all of the neighboring gardens,
And to-day we have naming of parts.

This is the lower sling swivel. And this
Is the upper sling swivel, whose use you will see,
When you are given your slings. And this is the piling swivel,
Which in your case you have not got. The branches
Hold in the gardens their silent, eloquent gestures,
Which in our case we have not got.

This is the safety-catch, which is always released
With an easy flick of the thumb. And please do not let me
See anyone using his finger. You can do it quite easy
If you have any strength in your thumb. The blossoms
Are fragile and motionless, never letting anyone see
Any of them using their finger.

And this you can see is the bolt. The purpose of this
Is to open the breech, as you see. We can slide it
Rapidly backwards and forwards: we call this
Easing the spring. And rapidly backwards and forwards
The early bees are assaulting and fumbling the flowers:
They call it easing the Spring.

They call it easing the Spring: it is perfectly easy
If you have any strength in your thumb: like the bolt,
And the breech, and the cocking-piece, and the point of balance,
Which in our case we have not got; and the almond-blossom
Silent in all of the gardens and the bees going backwards and forwards,
For to-day we have naming of parts.

NOTE: This antiwar poem has the perfect balance of contrasting sounds and images, all supported by the structure with the break within each stanza occurring in the middle of line 3. The death (or masturbatory) imagery at the start of each stanza is contrasted with the life giving imagery in the end of each stanza. READ ALOUD and enjoy.

THEMES

THEMES (175) are those major ideas that the author is concerned about. A partial list of recurring THEMES includes GOOD vs. EVIL; APPEARANCE vs. REALITY; The INDIVIDUAL and his/her relationship to GOD, NATURE, COMMUNITY (or STATE as a special case of community), SELF, &/or FAMILY; Also MATURITY; GUILT; RESPONSIBILITY; IDENTITY, and others. Themes that are specific to the novel LOVE MEDICINE include alcoholism, the Ojibwa culture vs. the Roman Catholic (or White) culture, Life on the reservation vs. city Life, child and spousal abuse, & Vietnam. In Nathaniel Hawthorne's short story, "Young Goodman Brown (see 10.4.1, below)," and Oliver Stone's movie, PLATOON (see 10.2.8, below), the authors both treat the themes of a maturing protagonist, and Appearance vs. Reality. Stories with recurring themes and plots (Here, a young man goes into the woods/jungle and confronts the forces of evil), are called METASTORIES. Note the similarities of plot and theme between Disney's THE LION KING and Shakespeare's HAMLET-they are virtually the same story, but with a different setting.

PLOT/STRUCTURE

PLOT or STRUCTURE (9) refers to the order of events in a work. In addition to the chronology, the causation, may be very important. A great story, like a great life, usually has a beginning, a middle, and an end. INTRODUCTION, COMPLICATION (The interacting of characters and events), CLIMAX, FALLING ACTION OR DENOUEMENT, and RESOLUTION are terms that we often use in analyzing PLOT or STRUCTURE. A Shakespearean play normally has five acts, with the Introduction occurring in Act 1, the Rising Action or Complication in Acts 2 and 3, followed by the climax in Act 4, and the Falling Action and resolution occurring in Act 5. Most stories are told in linear, chronological fashion, from the perspective of one narrator. But LOVE MEDICINE, like Faulkner's AS I LAY DYING, is an episodic novel-or a book of episodes, which, seemingly has little plot.
SETTING: Place, Time, Weather, Props

SETTING (92) is the context of the work. Where does it take place? What is the weather? What is the time of day or night, or the time frame? What props or other items are introduced? The stick of the old man (Devil?) in "Young Goodman Brown" is a good example of the latter, or the sewing needle that keeps going through the ear of Tang Ao in Maxine Hong Kinston's "On Discovery." A poem set in the Maine woods (Edwin Arlington Robinson's "New England") brings different assumptions than the tale of the Trung Sisters set in Viet Nam.
IMAGERY/Tone/Diction

IMAGERY (or DICTION) (588) are the word pictures or language used in the work. IMAGERY is particularly critical in poetry. The TONE of the language in a novel or short story is normally important. In Albert Camus' THE STRANGER, the imagery in the latter part of the novel is that of incarceration; the tone is that of a detached, indifferent protagonist. Word choice, or Diction, also influences the TONE of a work. The language in PULP FICTION is different in tone from that of Truman Capote's great story about a boy, his kite, and an older woman who befriended him, "A Christmas Memory." Images may be images of sight, smell, touch, or hearing. Images may be metaphors (Nguyen is a deer.) or similes, comparisons using the terms "like" or "as." (Nguyen is like a deer.)

CHARACTER/CHARACTERIZATION

CHARACTER & CHARACTERIZATION. Characters are the people (or animals) in the story or poem. We can think of them as the MAIN character or PROTAGONIST, MAJOR CHARACTERS, or MINOR CHARACTERS. In Flaubert's MADAME BOVARY, Emma is the PROTAGONIST, Emma and Charles and Homais are the MAJOR CHARACTERS, and Hippolyte is a minor character. Think, however about the THEME developed by Hippolyte's operation. CHARACTERIZATION refers to HOW characters are developed.

Characters may be further categorized as major or minor, flat or round, or foils, characters who exist in order to tell or show us things about another character. (see 10.4.9 Forrest Gump, below).
POINT OF VIEW

POINT OF VIEW refers to WHO is telling the story (or who is the speaker in poetry). Point of View is generally FIRST PERSON, in which a character tells the story, or THIRD PERSON in which an outsider tells the story. The THIRD PERSON may be omniscient, knowing everything, including character's minds, and able to move to the past or present, or future. The third person may or may not be objective, or his omniscience might be limited to one character. (In a few rare cases, the narrator may be a liar—what we typically call an unreliable narrator.) The answer to the question of who is (are) the narrator(s) in John Crowe Ransom's poem "Bells for John Whiteside's Daughter" is critical to the development of the author's THEME, and your understanding.

WRITING ABOUT LITERATURE

By looking at the parts and pieces of a literary work we are able to put them back together into a whole with a far greater appreciation for the THEMES of the work itself. This will heighten our understanding and therefore the MEANING of the work to our own lives. To effectively write about literature we may ARGUE how an element contributes to a THEME, or we might do a CLOSE READING of a representational passage. As always in effective writing, we want to think small and RESTRICT. A detailed analysis of a minor character is preferable to a surface analysis of a major character.

SAMPLE PAPERS

Paragraph on "Mr. Green" by Lucia F.

In 'Mr. Green' Butler develops the theme of a woman's self-discovery through the use of a plot that illustrates the inner conflicts she feels because of her traditional Vietnamese upbringing. The structure of the story unfolds throughout the life of the protagonist from a child living in Vietnam to middle adulthood living in America. The story is told in first person through the point of view of the main character. In the setting of a family environment, a female, the protagonist, maintains a close relationship to two antagonists, her grandfather, and a parrot, who symbolizes family and the passage of time. While a child, the female develops conflicts with the harsher aspects of being Viet namese. Her grandfather is the catalyst for her struggles with religion, gender, and death. In the story, she becomes invalidated for being female when her grandfather tells her that she cannot worship ancestors because she is not male. She also learns that her Catholic religion is less than admired by her grandfather. Her struggles become more complex when she acknowledges her first experience with death. Her grandfather takes her to the market to purchase some sparrows, brings them home, and she learns from her mother how to twist the heads to prepare them for dinner. Eventually, her struggles are further complicated by the experience of her grandfather's illness and death. In adulthood she provides care for Mr. Green, the parrot bequeathed to her from her grandfather. It is while she is caring for this parrot that she comes to realize that her current struggles are due to conflicts from the past; mainly because of her grandfather. I believe the climax of the story is when she realizes that her grandfather, while dead, continues to influence her conflicts through the life of the parrot. The parrot symbolizes the presence of her grandfather and eventually she kills the parrot when the first signs of its impending death are near. By swiftly ending the parrot's suffering, the act symbolizes her deeper self realization and self acceptance.

A Walk in the Woods by Kathy G.

"Had Goodman Brown fallen asleep in the forest, and only dreamed a wild dream of a witch meeting?" (Hawthorne 71) This is a concluding question in the short story "Young Goodman Brown" written by Nathaniel Hawthorne. Were the events of the night actual or a dream? Real or not? Brown receives a shocking blow in this story when he becomes aware that people, whom he has revered his entire life, are not what they appeared to be. Appearance can be an unreliable measure. In "Young Goodman Brown," the author uses point of view to help develop the theme of appearance vs. reality. I say this because the author chose a non-omniscient, third person to tell his story. This speculative narrator uses words that contribute to an atmosphere of uncertainty, while he intentionally fosters ambiguity by presenting two interpretations of the same event.

The use of a nonparticipant narrator, who stays with Goodman Brown from beginning to end, provides a reliable witness to the events that take place, while his lack of omniscience adds to the mysterious nature of the story. Although he does not know everything, he can see into Brown's mind and he lets the reader know what this character is thinking and feeling. For example, when Brown decides not to go any further into the forest, the narrator tells us, "The young man sat a few moments, by the roadside applauding himself greatly and thinking with how clear a conscience he should meet the minister..."(201). Or, at the beginning of the story we are given: " 'Poor little Faith!' thought he, for his heart smote him" (197). Most information, though, comes to us from conversations and from descriptions of the characters and the events as they unfold. Since Hawthorne uses the third person the reader gets a more reliable rendering of this trip into the forest than if it was told by the emotionally involved main character. By way of this calm and impartial narrator, the reader actually sees more than Goodman Brown does, as Brown is distracted by his own feelings as things are revealed to him. When the devil throws down his staff at Goody Cloyse's feet "where, perhaps, it assumed life," Brown misses seeing it because he is so astonished by the revelation that Goody Cloyse knows this evil man, he looks away for a moment (Hawthorne 200). The mysterious occurrences are more believable coming from the witness, which makes them even more mysterious. The reader can not dismiss his observations as those of an unbalanced or distraught main character; he is just reporting what he sees, or at least what he thinks he sees. Or is he?

The narrator uses words and asks questions that cause the reader to feel uncertain about what is really happening. Words like "might," "appeared to," "seemed to," "perhaps," "as if," "fancied," "might almost," and "were such a thing possible," are used to describe events, creating doubt on the part of the reader and a desire to know what is real. When Brown's companion bursts out laughing, the narrator tells us he shook so hard "that his snake-like staff actually seemed to wriggle in sympathy," causing the reader, again, to question whether the staff might actually be a serpent (this was the second time it was mentioned in the story) (199). He did not say the staff "actually wriggled," which would imply that it did, or "seemed to wriggle," which implies that it just looked like it did, but "actually seemed to wriggle," which falls somewhere closer to saying it did, but not quite. The reader finds himself squinting his eyes trying to see it for himself. The speaker also asks questions that he never gives the answers to. When the devil was about to dip his hands in the baptism bowl, the narrator asks, "Did it contain water reddened by the lurid light, or was it blood? or perchance a liquid flame?" (205) The reader will never know. And the narrator only gets trickier.

Throughout the story, he teases the readers by presenting two interpretations of the same event. One of the best examples of this is the first description of the staff belonging to the man Goodman Brown met in the forest "which bore the likeness of a great black snake, so curiously wrought, that it might almost be seen to twist and wriggle itself, like a living serpent. This, of course, must have been an ocular deception assisted by the uncertain light" (198). Is the staff twisting or is it an illusion? Another example is the horses and riders in the woods. Goodman Brown hears the hoof-tramps of horses and can hear the voices of the riders. The sounds appear to be "within a few yards of the hiding place; but owing, doubtless, to the depth of the gloom" the riders and horses can not be seen" (201). Are they invisible, or is it too gloomy to see them? We simply do not know. When the narrator uses the words "this of course must have been" and "but owing, doubtless," offering pat explanations for these strange circumstances, he actually increases the reader's curiosity and doubt. "These ambiguities he conveys and fortifies by what Yvor Winters has called 'the formula of alternative possibilities,' and F.O. Matthiessen 'the device of multiple choice,' in which are suggested two or more interpretations of a single event....This device of multiple choice, or ambiguity, is the very essence of Hawthorne's tale" (Fogle 16). And he uses the narrator to accomplish this task.

Nathaniel Hawthorne chose a third person, non-omniscient narrator to tell this story. The speaker uses words that cause uncertainty and he teases the readers by offering more than one interpretation of a single event, in order to create ambiguity that is central to the story's theme. In "Young Goodman Brown," the author uses point of view to help develop the theme of appearance vs. reality. We live in a society that thrives on appearances; and yet, it is near impossible to understand and attain insight into the actions and motives of others, Good or bad. In the story, the reader never can conclude if anything is real or not. It offers a great example of the consequences of disappointment and disillusionment one risks when judging by appearance.

Works Cited

D, Richard. Peer Editor. Cyber-classmate to the author of this paper. 17 May 2000.

Fogle, Richard Harter. HAWTHORNE'S FICTION: THE LIGHT & DARK. Norman: University of Oklahoma Press, 1952.

Hawthorne, Nathaniel. "Young Goodman Brown." LITERATURE: AN INTRODUCTION TO FICTION POETRY, AND DRAMA. Eds. X.J. Kennedy and Dana Gioia. 2nd compact ed. New York: Longman, 2000: 196-206.

S, John. Peer Editor. Cyber-classmate to the author of this paper. 18 May 2000.

W, Bill. Peer Editor. Cyber-classmate to the author of this paper. 20 May 2000.
PLATOON (Academy Award,1986, Best Picture)

A young man, Chris Taylor, drops out of college and volunteers for Viet Nam. He is white, well-educated, and naive. In the setting of the jungle he meets the contrasting forces of good in Sgt Elias (a Christ figure--note the biblical name and the crucifixion imagery when Elias, played by Willem Dafoe, is killed) and the forces of evil in Sgt Barnes (note the scar, the image of evil, on the face of this character played by Tom Berenger.) Initially blamed for a blown ambush in which he is wounded, Chris returns to the unit and his soul is torn between the two camps in the Platoon. After he realizes that Barnes has caused the death of Elias by shooting him and then lying about it, Chris resolves to kill Barnes, but not before the great battle (based on the actual battle of Suoi Cat). After he kills Barnes, who dares him to, Chris leaves the jungle setting on a helicopter, resolving to tell "The World" about the meaning of Viet Nam, namely that we were our own enemy, and defeated each other. I personally believe the climax of the story is not when Tayler kills Barnes, but earlier when he broke up the rape in the village, just after he had been as evil as he ever was in shooting at the feet of the mentally handicapped, one legged boy--that seems the irrevocable turning point. The Point of View is often First Person, with an interior monologue done in voice over. This is virtually the same tale as Hawthorne's "Young Goodman Brown," but with a happier ending. (Not in PLATOON, Chris Taylor eventually became a community college teacher, with his own televised course about Viet Nam.)

FORREST GUMP

Another Oscar-winning Best Picture (PLATOON won in 1986), FORREST GUMP has a flat major character, he of the title. The flatness derives from the mental retardation (IQ of 75), nicely set against Jenny, the girl he met going to first grade on the bus. Jenny goes through much character development throughout the movie. Other major characters include Forrest's mother, Bubba, and LT Dan Taylor. The movie covers the American cultural waterfront with an allusion to Herman Melville's MOBY DICK in the scene in which Gary Sinise (LT Taylor) rides out a storm lashed to the mast, and goes from that historical starting point-and the concurrent joke of Forrest's being named for Gen Nathan Bedford Forrest, the founder of the Ku Klux Klan, all the way to Viet Nam, and Jenny's sadly dying of AIDS. My 84 year- old father-in-law said it was the greatest movie he had ever seen. I concur.

I wonder where my own movie, FIRE BIRDS, comes in--it, like TOP GUN, is heavily based on the meta story in WINGS, the first (1928) Best Picture winner. If Paramount had only let us reuse the title. ...

"Yes, he thought, between despair and nothing, he would take despair." Wm. Faulkner

Summary

THEMES are developed by an author and are major ideas with which s/he are concerned. MEANING is the personal significance of the work to YOU, given your particular universe. An author might develop alcoholism as a theme; the meaning of that theme to you may be colored by your having a friend or relative who is an alcoholic.

Authors develop THEMES using PLOT or STRUCTURE, SETTING, CHARACTER & CHARACTERIZATION techniques, IMAGERY (or tone or diction), and POINT OF VIEW. You will be asked to evaluate literature using these terms.

You can begin to evaluate poetry by asking the question, "How does a Poem Mean?" IMAGERY, SOUND, and STRUCTURE are the major elements of Poetry, and you should also ask the questions: "Who is the Speaker?' and "What is the Occasion?" Recurring THEMES are noted above. The key to effective writing about literature is to think small, and restrict. Write about a minor character, not a major one. Develop one theme, or one element, but do not try too much. Focus is the key.

THE ELEMENTS OF LITERATURE: SLIDES

THEMES

- Major Ideas of the Author

- Created by the conscious use of the (five) elements of literature: Plot/Structure, Setting, Imagery (including tone and diction), Character/Characterization, and Point of View

THEMES include

- Good vs. Evil

- Appearance vs. Reality

- Maturity

- Guilt

- Responsibility/Gender Roles

- Identity

- The Individual and her/his relationship to

- God

- Nature

- Family/Community

- Self

- etc

WHY READ LITERATURE?

- Note the Identity Question involved in The Individual and theme

- Understanding of Others

- Vicarious experience

- Measure of own Growth--Every Ten Years (example: THE DEERHUNTER)

The Elements of Literature

- PLOT/STRUCTURE
- SETTING

Unit 10 93

- IMAGERY (and tone, diction)
- CHARACTER/CHARACTERIZATION
- POINT OF VIEW

PLOT/STRUCTURE

- Good Works normally need a Beginning, Middle, End
- FIVE (5) Elements of Classic Plot:

Introduction,

Complication or Rising Action,

Climax,

Falling Action or Denouement,

Resolution

SETTING - The Context

- Where does it take place?
- What is the time frame, seasons, or time?
- What is the weather?
- What props or other items are introduced?

IMAGERY: Word Pictures

- Include the senses: sight, smell, taste, touch, hearing
- Focus on types: Nature Imagery, Weather imagery, Battle imagery, Sports imagery, Love Imagery
- Metaphors

- Similes (use "like" or "as")
- Consider also TONE and DICTION

CHARACTER/CHARACTERIZATION

.CHARACTER- The people (or animals) in a story

- Protagonist (Main character, e.g. Kieu)

- Major characters, minor characters, flat characters, round characters.

- CHARACTERIZATION: HOW the character is developed

POINT OF VIEW

- WHO is telling the story?

- FIRST PERSON: a character tells the story

- THIRD PERSON: An outsider tells the story

- THIRD Person may be omniscient, or have limited omniscience; may or may not be reliable
The ELEMENTS (review)

- PLOT/STRUCTURE

- SETTING

- IMAGERY (and tone, diction)

- CHARACTER/CHARACTERIZATION

- POINT OF VIEW
THEMES (review)

- Good vs. Evil

- Appearance vs. Reality

- Maturity

- Guilt

- Responsibility/Gender Roles

- Identity:

- The Individual and her/his relationship to:

- God
- Nature
- Family/Community
- Self
- Other characters not previously named.

I hope you enjoyed and learned from this text. Stay proactive with your education. Comments/questions to the author at swenssonjohn@gmail.com

LAST THOUGHT: Wear your SEATBELTS and NO DRUGS!!

www.ingramcontent.com/pod-product-compliance
Lightning Source LLC
Chambersburg PA
CBHW080324170426
43193CB00017B/2901